VALENTIA.
A DIFFERENT IRISH ISLAND.

by
NELLIE O'CLEIRIGH

Portobello Press.

Portobello Press,
38 Templemore Ave.,
Rathgar.
Dublin 6.

Published in Ireland by Portobello Press 1992.

Copyright (c) Portobello Press 1992
ISBN 0 9519249 0 7
Valentia. A different Irish Island.

Printed and bound by Colour Books Ltd, Baldoyle Ind Est. Co. Dublin

Cover illustration by Malcolm Sowerby.
Cartography by Michael Beary.

Publisher: Niall O Cleirigh
Editor: Nessa O'Mahony

Acknowledgements

Because I am not a native islander, I may not be the best person to write an account of life on Valentia. We have had a house on the island for 22 years and since 1985, when I opened "Crafts and Curios" I have spent every summer there, so perhaps I can be counted as an islander by adoption.

I dedicate the book to Tessa O'Connor, who created the superb Heritage Centre in Knightstown. She very generously gave me access to all the material she had collected there. We shared many hours in the various archives in Dublin and got great pleasure from our work. I cannot thank her sufficiently.

I wish to express my thanks to all the institutions who gave me permission to reproduce from their material, the National Library, Dublin, the Public Records Office, Dublin, the State Paper Office, Dublin, the Quaker Library, Donnybrook, Dublin, the Royal Irish Academy, Dublin, Trinity College, Dublin, and Kerry County Library, Tralee, Co. Kerry. A special "thank you" is due to Adrian FitzGerald who gave me access to the FitzGerald family papers and who told me where to locate most of the FitzGerald papers in Irish archives. Tom O'Neill, retired Professor of History from University College, Galway, and his wife, Marie, were most helpful in pointing out sources of nineteenth century Irish history. Marie Luddy of the University of Warwick gave me information about Helen Blackburn. Beatrice Dixon and her late husband, Freddie, allowed me to get copies of photographs as did Adrian FitzGerald. Former colleague Tom Duggan and Michael O'Riordan of the Land Commission helped to give me access to the papers dealing with the FitzGerald and Trinity College Estates. Eilis Dillon was most helpful and encouraging.

The photographs are the work of David Cockroft, Mrs Doreen Kelliher, Adrian Mackey, Conor O'Cleirigh, and the late Mike Shea. Quite a number are from the Lawrence Collection.

        The cover, by Malcolm Sowerby, is by kind permission of Mrs Judy Malcolm.

        It is impossible to list all the islanders who gave me accounts of life on Valentia. I hope that anyone who is not mentioned in the credits at the back of the book will forgive me. I would like to pay special tribute to Mrs Hanoria O'Shea, who gave me such a detailed account of women's lives. John William O'Sullivan of the Ring Lyne in Chapeltown, was most helpful in suggesting older islanders who might have information about the seine fishing.

        Without the help of my "Committee" it would not have been possible to have dealt with the technicalities of publishing the book. To Niall, my thanks for removing all obstacles and coping with the technical details; to Nessa for all the work of editing; to Maryrose, Conor, Fiona and Shane for candid comments and help; to Michael Beary for suggestions and for the excellent maps. To Cormac, my thanks for help and for putting up with it all so patiently.

Nellie O'Cleirigh
Dublin
April 1992

To Tessa.

Contents

Chapter One
Introduction

Valentia is approached from Cahirciveen along the beautiful Iveragh Peninsula, just off the Ring of Kerry. About seven miles by three, it houses the most westerly community in Europe. Its three hills form a spine along the length of the island, with high cliffs on the west and fields sloping down to the sea where it faces the mainland. Today, there are less than 700 inhabitants, who earn a living from farming, fishing and tourism. There is also a radio station, a small factory and a boat-building business. Valentia has not been an island since the opening of the bridge at Portmagee in 1970 which joined it to the mainland.

There is very little documentary evidence of life on Valentia before the eighteenth century but we know it was inhabited in very early times. The superbly preserved "fulachta fiadh" (cooking place of the deer or of the wild), which are found in the bog at Culloo and at Imlagh, have been carbon-dated to prove that people lived there in the Pre-Christian era. The "ceiliunachs" or early burial grounds for unbaptised children, with their crosses and incised stones, which are scattered round the island, are all signs of early occupation.

According to the first known written record of occupation, *Taxation of Pope Nicholas*, about 1291 AD a church on the island was valued at or taxed at 13/4d. In 1300, the Irish Chieftain, Turlough O'Conor, brought a fleet to Desmond, West Munster, and plundered Dairbhre (the early name in Irish for Valentia meaning the island of the oaks).

Trade with Spain was important. A shipment from Valentia Harbour in 1569 amounted to "2,000 beeves (cattle), with cargoes of skins and tallows". The cargoes coming back from the Continent would appear

1

to have been mainly wine and salt like that from Andalusia which was recorded in 1580. There was also a story of a wine auction on board ship between Portmagee and Valentia, where the local gentry came to collect their supplies and the Revenue Officers turned a blind eye to the proceedings, presumably sharing part of the cargo.

Even the townland names have not changed much from the early times. On a map dating from about 1600 preserved in the Lambeth Library in London, they are spelled Corabeg (Coarhabeg), Corremore (Coarhamore), Tinne (Tinnies), Feahmah (Feaghmaan), Glanlim (Glanleam), and are located roughly where these townlands are shown on the Ordnance maps today.

In the sixteenth century the island formed part of the lands of McCarthy More, who had ousted other Irish families, the Falveys and the O'Sheas. Between 1612 and 1641 it belonged in part to Peter and John Hussey and in 1653 the Hussey lands were forfeited and granted to Lord Annesley with those of Daniel Oge McCarthy and Peter Connell. The Annesleys, who later took the title of Viscount Valentia, continued to own most of the island until the end of the eighteenth century, when it was leased and later bought out by the FitzGerald family, the Knights of Kerry.

The other major landowner on Valentia was Trinity College, Dublin, which obtained two townlands, Cool and Tinnies, when they were confiscated for treason. The lands were granted "by Letters Patent under Irish Grand Seal of 28th June 1597 at a rent of 16/- per annum and previously in the occupation of Taddeus alias Teige Dyalterie of Tyny attainted for treason". The lands of Cool and Tinnies formed part of a very large estate including the town of Cahirciveen and the village of Portmagee, which were the property of Trinity College.

In the last century the island was a very busy place and before the Great Famine had a population of just under 3,000. It had three major industries, fishing, slate quarrying and communication; it was the European Terminus of the first Trans-Atlantic Cable. Of these, fishing was the only occupation common to other Irish islands or to the coastal counties. What made Valentia a different Irish island was the development of the large slate quarry at Geokaun and the choice of the island as the terminus for the first Trans-Atlantic Telegraph Station. The slate quarry, which was opened in 1816, was a labour-intensive industry lasting almost one hundred years and providing employment for 500 people at its height. The first cable was

landed on the island 40 years after the opening of the quarry and it brought
a totally different style of "industry" which also lasted a long time, just
over one hundred years. There are very good surviving records to show
what life on the island was like in the nineteenth century. This book has
been compiled from these records and the recollections of the older
islanders.

Because the FitzGerald family, the Knights of Kerry, who owned
most of the island, left superb records, perhaps their side of the story may
seem to dominate but they were resident landlords and very much part of
island life and folklore.

Today, the island has two villages, Chapeltown and Knightstown.
The first is the older; in the early nineteenth century it was the only village
on the island and contained the island's Catholic church until Knightstown
Church was built in 1913. It also had the earliest National School as well as
a mill.

Knightstown was built because a processing yard and harbour were
needed to export the slate from the great quarry at Geokaun. It is a laid-out
village, designed by the Scottish engineer, Alexander Nimmo, at the
request of the Knight of Kerry. It was built in the early years of the last
century and is typical of a laid-out landlord's village. When the island was
at its most prosperous, early this century, Knightstown had a good hotel,
the Cable Station, the Slate Yard, two churches, a hospital, a courthouse, a
jail, a police barracks, a Mason's Lodge, a Fisherman's Hall, and several
prosperous shops including a bakery. A photograph of the wide main street
at this period shows two of the spacious shops on the left, with the police
barracks and the Court House, the single-story cottage on the right.

The island had two golf courses and a branch of the Agricultural
Bank, which was a co-operative. It had the benefit of resident Catholic and
Church of Ireland clergy, two doctors, a veterinary surgeon, several
schools, and a justice of the peace. Most important of all, Valentia had a
resident landlord, the Knight of Kerry.

At this period it was an island of two cultures, the Irish-speaking
area from Chapeltown to Bray Head and the English-speaking Knightstown
and its hinterland. Even the air was different once the hill above
Knightstown was crossed. The smell of the coal fires burning in the Cable
Station and the Lightkeepers' houses in the village was replaced by the turf
smoke from the rural houses.

The island population included a large community of farmers and fishermen, smaller farmers often being fishermen as well. There were many cottiers (men who occupied only a patch of ground on which to grow potatoes and who worked as labourers when they could get work). When the quarry was working it provided much needed employment. The staff of the Cable Station were the next largest group but there were also coastguards, lighthousekeepers, and the staff of the Wireless station. These, with the merchants and shopkeepers, the tradesmen and craftsmen, combined to make Valentia unique among Irish islands.

Even today, visitors to Knightstown are amazed to find terraces of fine Victorian and Edwardian two-storeyed houses in a laid-out village, with a clock tower facing a Royal Hotel.

Main Street, Knightstown Village early this century.

Chapter Two
The Knights of Kerry.

When islanders today talk about "the Knight", they are usually referring to Maurice FitzGerald, the 20th Knight who was the last Knight to reside permanently in Valentia, or his father, Peter, the 19th Knight. But there were four Knights involved with Valentia, Robert the 17th Knight (1716-1781), Maurice the 18th Knight (1772-1849), Peter FitzGerald the 19th Knight and the first baronet (1808-1880) and the second Maurice, the 20th Knight (1844-1916). This Maurice resided most of the year at Glanleam, on Valentia, until shortly before the start of negotiations for the sale of his 4,291 acres to the Congested Districts Board in 1910, which in turn sold it to the tenants.

The FitzGeralds retained their residence, Glanleam, until the 1930s and they also held on to the untenanted land around Glanleam House and quite a number of houses and cottages which the Congested Districts Board was unwilling to purchase.

The FitzGeralds were a Norman family who had held considerable areas in Munster. After the battle of Callan, in 1261, their title "Knight of Kerry" was created at the same time as the "White Knight" and the "Knight of Glin." John of Callan conferred these titles on his three natural sons and saw to it that each had an estate in keeping with his title. Gilbert, first Knight of Kerry, had his lands in Corca Dhuine, in the Dingle Peninsula, around the present town of Dingle and westwards to Ventry. The family had become Church of Ireland by the time they became involved with Valentia.

The earliest reference to FitzGerald presence on the island was in 1752 when the family leased land from the Annesley family for three lives, such a lease being a common method of letting land. This land was later purchased.

Robert, the 17th Knight, who was the first Knight to own part of Valentia, introduced linen manufacture to the island but he claimed in a letter dated 29th January 1771 that it advanced very slowly because the members of the Linen Board did not "extend their influence beyond the limits within which the members of the Board are immediately interested". The fact that Valentia was so remote from either Dublin or London did not deter Robert from seeking a seat on the Linen Board and he claimed, and probably rightly so, that it was principally owing to his efforts ".. that this western county has for many years past received any encouragement from it". Flax growing was relatively common in Kerry at this period.

Robert FitzGerald, 17th Knight of Kerry.

Robert's son, Maurice, the 18th Knight, was only nine years of age when his father died but Robert's widow lived on the island and brought up her family there, probably at Zelva, near where the ruin of the two-storey school-house building now stands, on the road from Chapeltown to Knightstown. The first house or cottage at Glanleam, later the family home, was built some time about 1820 but the FitzGeralds may not have lived all the time on the island as they had land at Ballinruddery near Listowel. Glanleam was enlarged during the last century. The present house is smaller than the original as part was taken down during the 1930s.

Maurice, the 18th Knight, became a Member of Parliament in Dublin in 1795 before the Union of Great Britain and Ireland, when he was only in his early twenties. He commanded a detachment of the Kerry Militia and fought against the French at Killala in 1798. He served under Castlereagh, the mastermind of the Act of Union. Maurice kept up his friendship by writing many letters to him over the following years. After the Union, Maurice became an M.P. at Westminster in London. He served as Vice Treasurer in Wellington's Government.

Maurice's stay in Government was cut short by the fall of Wellington's party from power. Maurice favoured Catholic Emancipation but later quarrelled with Daniel O'Connell, known as the Liberator, the man responsible for obtaining Catholic Emancipation. Maurice and O'Connell probably quarrelled over the Bill to Reform Parliament. According to Emily FitzGerald, writing in the 1930s, the family considered that his support of Catholic Emancipation cost Maurice "many years of official life and salary".

At this period, Maurice may not have spent much time on Valentia. Daniel O'Connell opposed him and in the next election FitzGerald lost his seat. But Maurice kept up his connections with Government and where possible used them to get favours for Valentia and incidentally for himself. He wrote constantly to Wellington and even named the front walk "Wellington Place" when he employed Alexander Nimmo to design a new village at "the Foot", facing Reenard Point on the mainland. He called the village Knightstown after himself and two of its streets were named "Peter" and "Jane". Island folklore claims that these were called after the FitzGerald family but Adrian FitzGerald, the present heir, says that Jane was not a family name.

Maurice's travels took him further afield than Parliament in London. He went to Belgium in 1815 at the height of the Napoleonic Campaign because he was anxious "to see all that was going on there", to quote his granddaughter, Emily FitzGerald. The war must have been a very casual affair, because he actually saw the French Cavalry reviewed by the Duc de Berri. He commented: "I am afraid, if they are not better commanded than by him, they will not do much good." According to his granddaughter, he later attended the famous ball on the eve of Waterloo and was the first to bring the news of the victory at Waterloo to the anxious Cabinet in London, a feat normally credited to the Rothschilds.

The improvements Maurice sought for the island were surprisingly varied. His efforts during the minor famine of 1823 and again during the Great Famine of 1847 are covered in the chapter on "Famine" and his involvement in the Slate Quarry is covered separately. He corresponded with Lord Lansdowne, with whom he was responsible for forming a committee to promote Valentia as a packet station for the North Atlantic, but nothing came of their efforts. Maurice actually envisaged Valentia as another Liverpool. Local lore credits him with being responsible for having the coastguards transferred from Portmagee to the island. As early as 1837 he applied for a lighthouse to be built at Cromwell Point on the island. He also wanted a lighthouse built on Bray Head and was in touch with the Admiralty about the necessity for a lighthouse on the Skellig Rocks.

Another favoured project was the setting up of an Agricultural College and, of course, he wielded considerable influence in the appointment of the Church of Ireland rector. When the rector, the Rev. Mr. Hewson, was promoted in 1847, Maurice wrote to Lord Clarendon at the Vice-Regal Lodge in Dublin who replied "I will not dispose of the living until I know whether you still desire it should be bestowed on the gentleman for whom you were at that time interested." Edward Sandiford was appointed in 1848, but we can only presume he was the candidate Maurice wanted.

Other correspondents were landlords like the Earl of Donoughmore at Knocklofty in Co. Tipperary, and politicians like Castlereagh and Cornwallis, who had commanded the British Army against the French in 1798; Maurice was in continuous contact with Castlereagh and Cornwallis.

Like so many Anglo-Irish families in Victorian times, the FitzGeralds encouraged visitors. Maurice had some famous visitors to the island, even during the Famine period. Lady Chatterton visited in 1838, the Duke of Rutland in 1848; Sir George Airy, Astronomer Royal, made several visits; Doctor Harvey, a famous botanist, came in 1844; Admiral

Ommaney, Arctic explorer, W.H. Russell, war correspondent, Sir Roderick Murchison, geologist, all came in 1847. Other visitors were Count Osalinski and Count Stralecki, who was very involved with famine relief. Lord Stanley (Earl of Derby) and Lord Tennyson came in 1848. Tennyson came in February, having visited the de Veres at Curragh-Chase in Co. Limerick. A note from Aubrey de Vere describing the visit said:

> He found there the highest waves that Ireland knows; cliffs that at one spot rise to 600 feet; fuchsias that no sea wind can intimidate; and the old Knight of Kerry who, at the age of nearly eighty, preserved the spirit, the grace, and the majestic beauty of days gone by, as chivalrous a representative of Desmond's great Norman House as it had ever put forth in those times when it fought side by side with the greatest Gaelic houses for Ireland's ancient faith and the immemorial rights of its Palatinate.

Tradition on the island is that Tennyson composed his immortal lines "Break, break, break, on thy cold grey stones, O Sea" during his visit to Valentia.

Maurice's first marriage to Maria La Touche, of the Irish banking family, brought him an estate in Carlow. The Carlow estate was smaller than the Valentia one but the land was better and had a higher rent per acre. Money inherited from an uncle also enabled him to buy back part of the Valentia lands in the Encumbered Estates Court. The purchase price, £28,145, was considered by the family to be high because "other Kerrymen bid us up".

But Maurice's finances were in considerable difficulty at his death in 1849. It would have been impossible for any Irish landlord to collect full rents during and immediately after the Great Famine of 1847 and his expenses in getting to and from London were high. There was the additional cost of maintaining an establishment in London and in those days Members of Parliament were not paid. His large family would also have been a considerable expense.

Maurice had many children but most of his sons predeceased him. His son Peter, who was 41 when he inherited the title in 1849, was actually his sixth son. Peter was already living on the island, presumably at Glanleam. He had been running the estate for some time, having previously lived in Cork where he had been agent for several landowners.

Peter FitzGerald, the 19th Knight, held the title for 31 years. His tenure covered the successful period of the Slate Quarry, the important years of the landing of the first Trans-Atlantic Cable, the Fenian Rising of 1867, the setting up of the Meteorological Office, and the royal visits of the Prince of Wales and Prince Alfred in 1858 and Prince Arthur Patrick in 1869.

Peter FitzGerald, 19th Knight of Kerry

Peter promoted the island as a base for the landing of the Cable and the setting up of the Cable Station and he remained in contact with the various people involved. He conducted a lengthy correspondence with the American promoter of the Cable, Cyrus Field, on the suitability of Valentia as the European terminus. Field wrote to the Knight in 1862 asking him to come to London to help in the negotiations with the British Government and suggested that their mutual friend, Mr. Crosbie, should come with him. He concluded his letter: "Europe and America must be joined by telegraph from Ireland to Newfoundland."

Not all Peter's efforts were well received. Carlisle, when Lord Lieutenant, the King's representative in Ireland, wrote from Dublin Castle, the seat of the British Government in Ireland, in February 1862: "I will consider whether I can put in a word about the Cable but it is quite obvious that the Government will really only be influenced by the opinion of experts upon the subject."

Lesser undertakings favoured by Peter were the installation of new advance storm warning signals invented by Admiral Fitzroy, and the trial of whale-boats for use as lifeboats. When the trials were carried out, one boat was manned by the coastguards and the other by local fishermen under Edward O'Neill.

The first lifeboat, the "Mary", came to the island in 1865, having been transferred from Renard on the mainland because only in Valentia could a competent crew be obtained. Peter FitzGerald became the Hon. Secretary to the Lifeboat Committee the following year. He also gave the site for the boat-house and an annual subscription.

Another local service sought by Peter was the extension of the Dispensary services on the island to all persons whose valuation was less than £3 under the Poor Law.

Peter was involved in setting out the garden at Glanleam. Pampas plants were a gift from A. Herbert of Muckross in 1865, at a time when the Herberts owned land on the island. The pampas growing at Glanleam today are presumably the descendants of this gift. At this period, the gardens possessed, besides many other beautiful shrubs, "the biggest fuchsia in the world". According to Peter's daughter, Emily FitzGerald, it was a Ricartonia which in 1865 measured over 300 feet in circumference, having for many years never been clipped or pruned. When it spread to the path that led to the lighthouse, iron arches were placed to carry the branches over the walk. Other exotic plants were imported around this time.

That Valentia was a remote island on the edge of the Atlantic did not stop Peter FitzGerald from keeping track of world affairs. He received an invitation to the funeral of the Duke of Wellington in 1852, presumably because of his father's friendship with the Duke. But his interests were not confined to English politics. The telegrams preserved among his papers include one informing him of the murder of President Lincoln at a New York theatre in 1865. Later, Bewicke Blackburn, who had been Manager of the Slate Quarry, sent him by telegraph what was practically a day-by-day account of the progress of the Franco-Prussian War. Many correspondents were asked for their photos and the family papers contain a set of studio photos of British politicians and prominent men of the day.

Rajah Brooke of Sarawak sent a photo in 1859. Numerous Irish landlords like Watson of Ballydarton in Co. Carlow, the Duke of Leinster, and Lord Dunsany, all sent photos and included in a list of "wanted photos" was Father Mathew, the apostle of temperance, who himself came from a landed family. Autographs were also asked for by Peter for his children and a witty letter from B.A.Gould, who was involved in the setting up of the observatory on the island, proffered autographs of American generals and admirals immediately after the Civil War as "generals were the most abundant crop on hands, thicker than leaves in Vallambrosa" and "Admirals may be had for the asking". Gould also provided a dissertation on American politics and information about the progress of the Canadian Pacific Railway. Another letter referred to solar eclipses, and of more local interest, to "the dredging expedition for shellfish carried out by the Knight". Gould also thanked the Knight for "pleasant evenings in your hospitable mansion" and "the affectionate happy domestic life in which your kindness admitted me to share and the romantic scenery of Bray Head".

Another project favoured by Peter was the building of the Killarney to Valentia Railway, something which didn't happen until after his death. A bridge to the mainland never seems to have been considered. According to Bernard Becker, a journalist who visited the island in 1880, Peter FitzGerald had attempted to establish a steam ferry to the island some years previously but it had been bitterly opposed by the ferrymen.

Peter FitzGerald was very involved in Church of Ireland affairs. Apart from local interest like the appointment of clergymen, both Church of Ireland and Catholic, he wrote numerous letters to the *London Times* including one in 1868 stating that "the Irish Church (Church of Ireland) is an injustice" and proposing "perfect religious equality to be obtained partly by levelling down the establishment and partly by levelling up the other churches". He even corresponded with one Edward de Bunsen on the amounts paid to the clergy in Germany. But Peter was not consistent. He did not approve of the Disestablishment because it would weaken the position of the Church of Ireland. In a letter to O'Brien of Cahermoyle, Co. Limerick, another resident landlord, he talked of "re-distribution" instead of "disestablishment".

Like his father, Peter was determined to have the Church of Ireland clergyman of his choice for Valentia. We have no way of finding out now how many candidates received the Knight's veto but one was certainly unacceptable, or to be more correct, his wife was not suitable because she was "uneducated and had no knowledge of music". Peter FitzGerald wasn't satisfied with controlling the appointment of the clergyman of his own Church. He also corresponded with Rev. Dr. Moriarty, the Catholic bishop of the Diocese, on the choice of the parish priest. Dr. Moriarty was known to be violently opposed to the Fenian Movement and so would have had some views common to the Knight. We can only presume that Rev. W. O'Reilly, who was appointed on the death of Fr. Kearney in 1875, met with the Knight's approval.

Peter's attitude to land was also probably slightly inconsistent. Like all landlords he feared any concessions to the tenants. He attempted to rationalise the rights of property, from a landlord's point of view. He also had some notion of the responsibilities and duties of landlords, at a time when most Irish landlords were absentees and were interested only in receiving their rents. Peter was very conscious of over-crowding and sub-division. He pointed out that if the available land on the island was divided up amongst the existing tenants and the landless men, they would each have so little that no one could make a living. Evictions and transfers of tenants during his lifetime are dealt with in detail in a later chapter.

Peter FitzGerald's period as Knight included the Fenian rising of 1867. He called his tenants together and, as a result of the meeting, an address of loyalty was sent to Queen Victoria. Presumably the tenants were afraid to oppose their landlord. Peter even threatened that if there were any Fenians on the island, the Cable Station might be removed elsewhere. In fact Peter's claim that there were no Fenians was proof that he certainly did not know everything that went on. *Leabhar Sheain Ui Connaill* gives a very vivid picture of Valentia Fenians training:

One of the O'Driscolls was their captain. They used to be on the summit of Valentia, where there is a level mountain, and every moonlight night all the boys of Valentia were drilling there. It was discovered that such things were going on, probably they had been spied on. O'Driscoll's house was come to in order to arrest him. A servant girl helped him to escape out the back door and he did not stop until he went to America.

The author heard later that the girl followed him to America and married him out there.

On at least one other occasion the islanders were able to outwit their landlord. The Knight had arranged for a group of them to go to Cahirciveen to cast their votes in an election for his chosen candidate and at this time there was no secret ballot. On the morning of the voting the ferry boat was conveniently not available, having run aground on a rock the previous evening. There were ways and means of getting one up on the landlord.

When the Knight was accused of instructing his Carlow tenants how to vote, he told Ball, the candidate for Carlow, that landlords should have the right to influence their tenants the same as anyone else! But Peter was better able to handle opposition than other landlords. The Earl of Kingston, who had a very large estate and who lived at Mitchelstown Castle, was driven insane when his tenants voted en masse against the candidate of his choice.

There were two royal visits to the island in Peter's lifetime. The first was in 1858 when Albert Edward, Queen Victoria's son, visited; there is a letter of thanks from him preserved among the FitzGerald papers. The second visit in 1869 is better documented. It brought publicity to Valentia and also gave the title "Royal" to the Hotel, which up to then had been simply "Mrs Young's". Prince Arthur of Connaught arrived with his equerry, Colonel Elphinstone, and a large retinue. Rooms had been booked at the hotel. The party arrived at Reenard on the mainland at 3pm on April 22nd.

The islanders in large numbers and wearing their holiday clothes, were waiting to give the Prince a hearty welcome. At a quarter to four, he landed amidst the vehement cheering of the people who followed him to the residence of the Knight of Kerry. A huge bonfire was lighted at 5 o'clock, and the Knight ordered barrels of porter to be given to the crowd. His Royal Highness then visited Young's Hotel (henceforth to be called the 'Royal').

The Prince returned to Glanleam for dinner at 7pm when he met a number of the notabilities of the island, invited for that purpose by Sir Peter. Among them was the Rev Thomas Maginn, 50 years parish priest of the island, who is remembered as being a "toady" of the Knight's.

Older islanders claim that two upstairs windows in the Hotel were said to be in "the King's room" and that the self-flushing Victorian toilets with coloured designs on them were put in specially for this royal visit or a later one.

It was intended that the Prince should visit the Skellig Rocks during his stay, but the "sea being high and His Highness a bad sailor", the project was abandoned. Instead he visited the Telegraph Station. He then went on a tour of the northern side of the island and by that route returned to the residence of the Knight of Kerry where a ball was improvised in the evening.

After the royal visit, A.J.Pritchard, Aide to His Majesty, sent to the Knight a Cypress grown from seed brought by the Duke from Mt. Sinai; this was presumably the most acceptable gift which could be sent to Valentia.

Even when he was old, Sir Peter was a marvellous letter-writer. The copies of his letters preserved in Tralee Library show that in 1877, only three years before his death, he dealt with the day-to-day running of the estate and his personal affairs. Unfortunately the copies were made in pen on very thin paper and the ink has faded badly in parts, but it is possible to decipher enough to show that Peter in January 1877 ordered coarse Indian meal, which he wanted crushed, from a firm of Spaight. This may have been the meal which was used to pay the workers in the Quarry. Other purchases were seed for turnips, carrots and rye grass,wheat, cement, lead and turpentine and these were to be delivered by a Clyde steamer calling to the island in 1878. The gardens at Glanleam were still being planted. Most of the botanical names of the list are not legible but oaks, elms, beech, birch, alder, Norway Maple, Silver Maple, larch, sycamore and ash were all ordered. Sydney Spender Clay wrote from Cannes giving measurements of growth of fuchsias and asking questions about the azaleas and camelias growing out of doors at Glanleam.

In July of the same year Peter was writing to the Board of Works for an advance of money for works in the Glebe area of Farranreagh. At this time, too, he was negotiating a very important purchase: the lands in Coarhamore townland from the Herberts of Muckross. The purchase money was to be "about £6,000" and he was going to borrow part of the purchase money. Perhaps this was the money he wrote about later that he owed his agent Mr. J. O'Driscoll (known locally as "Lord John") a sum of £1,000 being the remainder of a greater sum. The negotiations for the purchase were protracted and the Tralee Library papers do not show the eventual purchase price. This was about 1880 when there was a minor famine and conditions were very bad in the West of Ireland. Tradition is that things were bad on Valentia then and were made worse by the closure of the Quarry.

Other letters from Peter during this period were to the Burser of Trinity College for money to improve Reenard Pier, to the office of the Commissioners of Irish Lights about delivering coal to Valentia, the Calf and the Skellig Lighthouses, to Mr. Ross of the Royal Irish Constabulary in Cahirciveen about letting a house for an R.I.C. barracks on Valentia. This was the building that is today Walsh's shop in Knightstown. The rent was £25 per annum with later an additional garden of 2 acres for a further £5.

Another letter was to Captain Needham, the Agent for the Trinity College estate, asking how many Protestant farmers were on the College lands "for Parish purposes". Before the influx of the Trans-Atlantic Cable staff increased the Protestant population of the island, the number of Protestants was quoted at between 100 and 150.

The authoritarian power of a landlord at this period comes across very clearly. Piped water was being supplied to the Hotel, and to a Mr. Crosbie, J. O'Driscoll, and Slate Quarry houses. The Knight wrote in October 1877 to Mr. Magnus, "the tenant of the Quarries", reminding him that "the water pipes to your house are my property" and continuing "Need I say how very welcome you are to the use of them until I might be compelled to remove them which I think will not be the case".

Peter could on occasion use his influence on behalf of his tenants. He wrote to T. Reddington, G.P.O. London, looking for a post in the Post

Office Telegraphs for "Michael Connor of this island". He also kept a keen eye on the orders and accounts; he wrote a stiff letter to McKenzie's, Seed Merchants, in March 1878 because they didn't send exactly what he ordered in seeds. There were a number of letters to his son Maurice about his affairs. Two years before his death he was obviously concerned about "Robert's Settlement", "letting my wife have for her life the use of the La Touche estate", "my Carlow estate to be vested in Trustees" as well as arrangements for his lands at Ballinruddery.

Peter was created a Baronet in 1880, with the understanding that a peerage would follow, but he died a few months later. Perhaps the best tribute to Sir Peter and the most telling account of his life's work can be taken from the newspaper report dated 23rd April 1869, just after the Royal visit: "Indeed the worthy Knight would have concentrated in his individual self all the elements of a government, law-giver, and king, for as such he is looked up to by the inhabitants". No Irish tenants would have given this approval to any landlord but it is probably a fair assessment.

Maurice FitzGerald, who succeeded in 1880, had been born in 1844 so that, like his father, he was not young when he inherited. He had been to school at Harrow, as had his cousins the Spring-Rices, following in the family tradition. He then had a very successful career in the British Army, serving in the Ashanti War and in Canada. He received, on his return from foreign service and coming of age, a beautifully written address of welcome from his tenants, and there is a letter of thanks from him to the tenants dated September 1865.

Maurice's letters to his father in Valentia include descriptions of tennis parties and a shoot, so that his career in the army can not have been all hard work or service abroad. In 1874 he was dining with the Royal Family at Sandringham. He considered this a very important occasion because he sent home to Valentia the dinner menu for that day. Also in his father's papers is a very distinct photo of him on his polo pony. In 1874 he spent a great deal of time with His Royal Highness, Prince Arthur of Connaught, Queen Victoria's son, to whom he became Equerry. Letters to his father describe a visit to Cannes and he was obviously very proud of riding with the Prince to the opening of Parliament in London.

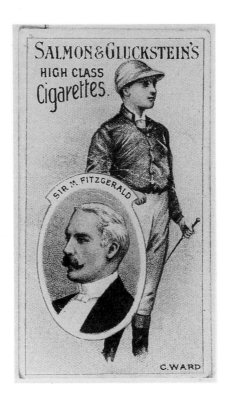

Sir Maurice FitzGerald, 20th Knight, racing enthusiast, featured on a cigarette card.

Maurice did not return to Valentia immediately on his father's death. The estate was managed by his brother Robert. Maurice did not resign his commission as Equerry until 1881, the year before he married Amelia Bischoffsheim, daughter of a wealthy Jewish banking family. Maurice would have been much more than an obscure Irish Knight at this time. His position as Equerry gave him an entree to Royal circles and presumably the Bischoffsheim money would have been welcome. The Valentia lands could not have provided much surplus income at this period. The 1880s were a time of minor famine and the beginning of the Land War so that it would have been difficult to collect rents on any Irish estate. His father's finances cannot have been very healthy at the end of his life because he had difficulty with the purchase of the Herbert's land on the island and this was the period when he owed money to his agent, "Lord John" O'Driscoll. However, from then on, the estate seems to have prospered and certainly money was poured into the house and the gardens. The FitzGeralds had joined the ranks of so many landowners, both Irish and English, who, at this period, married American heiresses or, as in this case, Austrian heiresses. Though Maurice and Amelia came to live on Valentia, they had houses in London and Newmarket, presumably provided by Amelia's wealth. Maurice did not sever his connections with the Royal Family. He was responsible for another royal visit, that of the Duke and Duchess of York in August 1897. Knightstown was bedecked with flags and evergreens for the occasion. Later, in 1901, Maurice went with Prince Arthur to the Durbar in India.

By 1911 the family had moved their permanent home to Buckinghamshire in England but the house at Glanleam was kept for holidays, maintained by a staff of four.

Maurice had a yacht, the Zelva, which was kept at Valentia and there was a seine boat for the family use. These boats provided jobs for local men as did the racing yacht, the Satanita, and later a second yacht, the Julna. The Satanita was large enough to sail to Cannes and other yachting destinations.   L 20,689 | 941-96

The FitzGeralds were very involved in horse racing as well as yachting at this period; horses called Sister Angela and Dozia both ran at Newmarket.

Lady Amelia FitzGerald's charities on the island included the establishment of a knitting industry, which will be described in greater detail in a later chapter. She was also involved in the hospital and it was under her auspices that the island hospital got free apparatus for the "Tallerman" treatment of rheumatism and kindred complaints.

The family were still influential in getting concessions for local people, though this time it seems to have been the wife who did the asking. In the FitzGerald papers preserved by the family, is one to Lady Amelia from Selbourne, appointing the son of McKew, a teacher on the island, as chaplain in the Royal Navy.

As late as 1912, Maurice was still interested in Irish affairs. In October of that year, the Irish Women's Franchise League sent a petition to the Lord Lieutenant on behalf of two English Suffragettes who were imprisoned in Mountjoy Jail in Dublin. The Knight of Kerry was among the signatories.

Maurice FitzGerald was already in failing health when the negotiations for the sale of the Valentia lands were started and when the family moved their permanent home to England. He died in 1915 but Amelia lived on until the 1930's.

The most interesting part of Maurice FitzGerald's involvement with Valentia is his dealings with his tenants.

The FitzGeralds did not fit into the classic description of "hunting, shooting, fishing" Anglo-Irish Landlords. There was no hunting anywhere near and the papers left by the family have no mention of organised shoots.

The FitzGerald family during the nineteenth century would have been regarded as very wealthy by their Valentia tenants, but both the first Maurice and his son Peter had very large families to provide for; to quote Adrian FitzGerald, the present heir to the title, "the Catholics were not the only ones with big families." The situation was also aggravated by the fact that there were three famines in their period. Probably only in the lifetime of Maurice the 20th Knight and his wealthy wife, Amelia, would they have been independent of rents from land. The rents from their Valentia estate, the Carlow estate, at one period a small estate in Co. Limerick, and the lands at Ballinruddery in North Kerry would not have totalled anything like the rents enjoyed by Lord Lansdowne and Lord Kenmare, who owned 94,983 acres and 91,080 acres respectively in Kerry.

Chapter Three
The Land.

The earliest description of life on Valentia dates from about 1709:

It is remarkable for little but its fruitfulness and the long life of its inhabitants, it being usual here to have men strong and healthful at four score or an hundred years old, in so much that some will jocosely assert that the sons are forced to bring out their old parents on the continent (as I may call it) of Ireland to die. Whether their length of days proceed from the wholesomeness of the air or from the careless lives of the inhabitants I shall not dispute but it's certain that no people in the world live more free from trouble and anxieties of this life than the inhabitants of this place, they have little to do, but put their corn into the ground and with patience expect a plentiful crop in which they are seldom or never disappointed.

And afterwards they sit down and eat it with temperance and frugality, luxury and variety of food (those enemies of the health and happiness of mankind) being never known in this place.

Some years later, in 1777, Trinity College lands, which totalled 789 acres, were described as "arable and pasture", "good mountain pasture", "bog", "mountain", "Heathy and Moory wet pasture" and "wet pasture".

From 1731 onwards these lands, with other lands, were leased for periods of 21 years to members of the Stoughton and Gun families, who came originally from Ballynoe and Carrigafoyle in Co. Kerry. These

21

families let the lands in small lots direct to tenant farmers. The final lease was for 21 years from 1st November. 1844 and, when this expired, Trinity College took over the management of the Valentia lands and appointed as its agent, Captain Needham. He had the distinction of being the only full-time agent ever employed by the College and was the manager of all its lands in Kerry and other areas of Munster. He was also the founder of the Masonic Lodge on Valentia.

Tradition on the island is that the Trinity tenants were much worse off than the Knight's tenants and this was certainly the Knight's own opinion when he declared that the Trinity tenants were "rack-rented".

Though the Knights of Kerry owned most of the island during the nineteenth century, they did not let all their land direct to the occupiers during that period. In the early part of the century large areas were leased to the O'Connells of Derrynane, the family of Daniel O'Connell, the Liberator. The O'Connells in turn rented to smaller tenants and, according to the Knights, allowed wholesale subdivision which resulted in fragmented holdings. When the lease fell in because of non-payment of rent, the FitzGeralds took over the management themselves and re-arranged the townlands.

In the middle of the last century the Knight of Kerry leased an area of 922 acres in Coarhabeg and 815 acres in Bray to the Spotswood family who resided at Coarhabeg. They in turn rented small areas of land to numerous tenants. The Spotswood lands included the village of Clynacartan which, like Craugh, has since disappeared. The Knight of Kerry re-possessed the lands about 1870 when, according to the Folklore Commission records, the Spotswoods became "briste", the word in Irish for "bankrupt".

After the purchase by the Knight of the townland of Coarhamore from the Herberts of Muckross about 1880, the entire island belonged to the FitzGeralds and to Trinity College until both estates were sold in 1913 to the Congested Districts Board, set up by the British Government in 1891 to investigate conditions in the West of Ireland.

The purchase price for the Knight's estate was £22,287. The Trinity College lands were sold as part of the College's total area of 9,895 acres in 29 townlands for £51,921. The Board advanced the purchase money to the tenants to enable them to buy out their holdings. Some re-arrangement and re-allotment was carried out by the Land Commission in the 1920s.

The population of Valentia was only 79 in the 1659 Census of Iveragh. This may have been a count of adult males only but even then the island could not have had more than a couple of hundred inhabitants. When the FitzGeralds first became owners, Robert, the 17th Knight, wrote in July 1770 about:

> an island in the Atlantick, mostly my own, circumstanced, as I have mentioned, in which there are several thousand acres of land naturally good, and above 800 inhabitants, naturally industrious, docile and well disposed but ignorant to a surprising degree.

Robert FitzGerald had introduced the growth of flax to the island and encouraged the making of linen but the island was still basically a corn-growing area, earning the name of the "granary of Kerry".

Some information about conditions on Valentia is gained from the report of the Poor Law Commission in 1836. They considered that many islanders were "small dispossessed tenantry" i.e. people who had previously been farmers. It was also noted that island labourers were better off than those in Tipperary, where the land was much richer. Islanders had plenty of fuel in the local bogs, they caught fish and those who were unable to fish could buy it cheaply; also they got milk.

By 1837 the island was exporting both corn and butter. Seven years later the "cash crop" was butter. James Butler, a local landowner, gave evidence in that year to the Devon Commission, one of the numerous committees set up by the British Government to collect information about the state of Ireland:

> As soon as a man has a son or a daughter grown up, the first thing he does is give them a bit of land. Very little corn for the market. In recent years the practice is to divide all farms. Land for letting is not advertised except by word of mouth.... There are such a number of bidders for it; there is not land sufficient to keep them in comfort and pay any reasonable rent; every man in the country generally offers more than the rent and therefore a sensible landlord will take the most solvent man and not look to the highest

rent.... I do not think there is any farm that gives more than 100 lbs of butter each cow in the season; that was admitted about 3 or 4 farms in the island of Valentia and 2 or 3 others.

Corn may have been grown in small quantities and pigs reared as well as cattle to produce butter for the cash to pay rent, but the crop grown to feed the islanders at this period was the potato.

Like the rest of Ireland, Valentia suffered a population explosion in the 70-80 years before the Great Famine. By 1837 the population had grown to 2,614 and to 2,920 by 1841 so that it would have needed a large amount of food to feed the people. It was estimated by another witness to the Devon Commission, Rev. Day, the Church of Ireland rector on the island, that 42 lbs of potatoes per day were needed to feed a labourer's family of two adults and three to four young children.

Potatoes grew on land which would not produce other crops and the actual food yield per acre was higher than corn but there were two great disadvantages. The potato crop rarely remained edible for a full twelve months, unlike corn which could be stored for years. Even more important was the fact that the potato was very vulnerable to blight, which could cause an entire crop failure. Even today the remains of the "lazy-beds" in which the potatoes were once grown can be seen on sloping ground on the island. All the cultivation was done with a spade and shovel giving work to the large class of landless labourers who lived on the island.

The lands were let according to "gneeves" or ploughlands, the right to graze a specific number of animals on a given area. In 1837 there were up to 300 small holdings varying from 1/2 a gneeve to 3 with a portion of bog and mountain. Though the local people talked in terms of "gneeves", the landlords kept all their records in the standard statute measure.

J.E. Butler, the Inspector for the Congested Districts Board, gave a detailed account of the island agriculture in August 1892. Small farms with a rateable valuation of less than £4 cultivated one acre of oats, 3/4 acre of potatoes, 1/4 of meadow and 1/4 of green crops. Just over a thousand acres of land for grazing was owned by the landlords and was let each year. All cultivation was by spade and shovel and the manures used were seaweed and sea-sand with some farm-yard manure. The breeds of Kerry cattle, sheep and poultry had been improved by Peter FitzGerald, the

19th Knight, and were better than usually found in that part of Co. Kerry. Labourers were employed on a casual basis in Spring and Autumn at about 2/- a day, an improvement on the 8d per day paid before the Famine. According to Butler, the people of Valentia were "fairly industrious and hard-working by fits and starts".

Islanders would hardly have agreed with this account of their lives. John McCarthy of Coarhamore gave a more detailed and human picture:

> Calf rearing was an important part of the economy. They sold yearlings or even at six months. On a 20 acre farm, 1 1/2 acres were used to grow oats, an acre for potatoes, which would feed a family of from eight to ten children and there was an awful lot of digging on an acre with a spade and shovel.

Early this century, mangolds and turnips were grown because they had more food value. Calves fed on these root crops had a better chance of surviving. A couple of acres in meadow for hay were a necessity, with some cabbage for the table and coarse big-headed cabbage for the cows. Rye was grown for thatching in the last century and later "fedduch", a wild grass like scutch.

When the potatoes were dug they were put into pits near the house, clamped on both sides with turf and tied down with old fishing nets. The mangolds pit was in the field and was also covered with turf and then straw. The cows were sometimes fed with sheaf oats in the winter but this was not considered good farming practice because much of the feed passed through the animal undigested.

Four cows and four calves had to be stall-fed during the winter. A pig was kept but few families could afford to kill the pig and salt it for home consumption. It was to be sold to pay the rent and later the Land Annuities. Finding money for the rent or rates, and later the annuities, was always a difficulty, though the annuities were considered a great improvement on the rents payable to the landlords. The annuities were the repayments to the British and later the Irish Governments for the money advanced to buy the land from the landlords.

A sow could also be fed on "casurbain", dandelion chopped with potatoes and yellow meal. Pollard, a type of meal, was bought for pigs and

25

even chickens. Furze for bedding cattle was another necessity, but each farmer could rent from the Knight and he got "as much as a man could cut in a day with a sythe (sic)" for 2/6d. A man who was a good mower (skilled in cutting with a scythe) was well paid and highly respected in the community.

The ferry boat: transport of farm animals from the island was never easy.

The island land lacked lime and so crops were not as good as they might have been. The evidence given to the Congested Districts Board after 1891 had various plans for bringing lime cheaply to the area but in fact sea weed, sea sand and cow manure were the main fertilisers, necessitating much back-breaking work.

The first tractor did not come to the island until after the Second World War and even wooden ploughs were a rarity, so that much of a man's time went to digging his land to prepare for planting and then reaping his harvest of hay and oats with a scythe. Cocks of hay had to be made and brought home by cart, tasks which took a long time. A farmer was lucky if he had a donkey, mule or jennet and a cart. The island branch of the Agricultural Bank lent money to buy carts. The establishment of the

Bank in 1903 was a great help to islanders and its able Secretary was the teacher, Daniel O'Sullivan. The presence of an Agricultural Bank on the island shows its relative prosperity at this period, because such banks were only set up in progressive areas.

The cart was a status symbol among farmers and one cart often went the rounds. It took three or four trips to bring one cock to the haggard. A man "of five or six cows" would have up to 20 meadow cocks to bring home and then these were all put into one large cock. The hay was cut out over the winter with a special knife, and it was important to secure the hay in the haggard properly against the gales that swept Valentia in the winter. Stacking oats was another chore. A man who had only four cows would need a stack of oats per cow and these were measured in "barts", from the Irish word meaning an armful. The base of the stack had to be constructed of furze because this would keep out rats and mice, the latter being the more destructive.

The Schedule of Areas prepared by the Knight's solicitor at the time of the sale of his lands to the Congested Districts Board gives some idea of the size of the farms. John Sugrue had 40 acres in Coarhabeg as well as an undivided share in 463 acres on Bray Mountain for which he paid a rent of £11 and he held his land on a Judicial Tenancy. He was comfortably off and had six cows. Of six farmers in this townland, three were described as "comfortable", one as "hardworking", and none owned more than 40 acres. A further six were described as fishermen who held from 13 to 46 acres, with various shares of mountain, and four were described as "poor".

Kilbeg West had one large farm, 54 acres held by John D. Bremner, who had a further 43 acres in Kilbeg East.

All the farms in Gortgower were less than 11 acres but Ellen Lynch, who occupied the largest, also had nine acres in Glanleam.

Coarhamore had the largest farms on the island at this period but the land there would not have been as fertile as in the middle of the island.

At that time J. Bourke was described as "a prosperous milk-farmer owning about 16 cows". He had won a prize for the best kept cottage on the island in a competition run by Kerry County Committee of Agriculture. In 1910 the Congested Districts Board Inspector wrote that the tenants as a rule were in very fair circumstances and had their holdings in fair order, but:

The island makes it very awkward for tenants to attend fairs or markets. Most of the dwellings were slated and in fair order; the rest are thatched and in poor order as a rule....The estate is well served by County roads as regards the tenanted lands, but the road to Bray Head requires to be repaired and extended.... There was not much drainage required on the east side of the estate but a good deal on the west side.... There was also sufficient turf on the island for the period when the annuities were being repaid.

Cutting the year's turf supply with a slean, turning it by hand to dry it, and bringing it home in baskets on women's backs was also a major yearly chore.

O'Donoghue's farmhouse in Feaghmann, reputed to be 200 years old.

Chapter Four
The Trans-Atlantic Cable.

For over a hundred years the Trans-Atlantic Cable formed an important part of the lives of those living on Valentia Island. Not only did the island become the terminus of the European end of the line but in the early years every message crossing the Atlantic passed through the Station at Valentia.

From 1842 onwards, experiments were carried out to transmit "electrical intelligence" under water through a cable. The idea of laying a cable across the Atlantic Ocean was first raised in 1854. The Atlantic Telegraph Company was formed in the United States and the financier Cyrus Field, one of its promoters and a friend of the Knight of Kerry, went to England to put the plan into operation. The cable was made at Greenwich and two ships were adapted to lay it. Electric cable had already been laid in the open sea, including from Dover to Calais in 1851 and later between Holyhead and Howth, but crossing the Atlantic was to prove a major challenge.

Valentia and Heart's Content in Newfoundland were chosen as termini because the shortest distance across the Atlantic was between these two points.

It was decided that one of the two cable ships, the Niagara, should land the shore end in Valentia and pay it out until her cargo was exhausted mid-way. The cable was to be spliced in mid ocean; from·there the other ship, the Agamemnon, was to lay the rest of the cable to Newfoundland. The first ship was provided by the American Government and the second by the British.

Even before the cable was landed on the island, the effects were already being felt. The first excitement on Valentia was in 1856 when the route for the cable was sounded by H.M.S. Cyclops, a small paddle-wheeler. The boat landed at Valentia and young John Lecky, son of the Quarry manager, recalled being brought on board by his father to meet the Captain. That year too, the British and Irish Magnetic Telegraph Co. got the contract for laying the land connection between Valentia and Killarney and thus into the national network. The original land connection went to White Strand on the mainland opposite the island, but in a short time the line was run across to Knightstown. Also the first administration buildings were erected on the island on the cliffs at Foilhomurrum, where the cable was to land.

While the shore work and the soundings were going on, the main preparations were also going ahead.

The Niagara and the Agamemnon, with their support ships H.M.S. Leopard and H.M.S. Cyclops from Britain and U.S.N.S. Susquehanna from America all met in Queenstown (Cobh) on 29th July 1857 and proceeded to Valentia, where on August 5th the shore end of the cable was brought in at Foilhomurrum cliffs. The occasion called for great celebrations on the island and even the Earl of Carlisle, Lord Lieutenant of Ireland, came from Dublin to Valentia to attend the "dejeuner" given by the Knight of Kerry to celebrate the occasion. The papers of the day sent journalists to cover the event but the most interesting description is given by John Lecky:

> To celebrate the laying of the cable, the Knight of Kerry gave a banquet and dance and these were held in John Driscoll's store in the Slate Yard. Most fortunately there were sufficient slabs ready to lay down for the floor and others for the dinner table; of course father again, he had trestles knocked up and the small slabs laid on them. What was done for seats I do not remember nor what the girls thought of the slabs for dancing on. However all went off splendidly. The tables cleared away and the floor was ready for the ball. At the upper end of the store the Knight wanted a big sheet with "Caith Mille Failthe" (sic) in Irish and evergreens all round. The evergreens were easy but the printing! Father again. He wanted a black paint that would dry quickly, so he had a happy thought, a huge bowl of starch was made into which he stirred gun-powder and so got his paint.

Whilst the banquet was proceeding I was sailing round in the "Helen" but on landing had a message from Father to come in to him. I sat between him and I think Sir William O'Shaughnessy, a great Indian Telegraph engineer. He gave me my first glass of champagne which I thought nice and Father gave me my first glass of claret which I thought nasty.... the next day was the servants ball.

John Lecky missed nothing by not being at the entire banquet. The speeches as reported in the newspapers were long, boring and very fulsome. Included amongst those present was Mr.Glass, the manufacturer of the main length of the cable.

The Great Eastern, the world's largest ship in 1865.

The most interesting visitor seems to have been Dr. Hamel, "a little old foreign gentleman" who was employed by the Russian Government to find out all the scientific information he could. There was no room for him at the Hotel, so Lecky Senior had a bed made up for him in the four-roomed garden house and he had his meals with the Lecky family. Apparently Dr. Hamel was an amusing visitor, but it was impossible to get any information out of him. He would not even tell the

Leckys how Russian leather got its distinctive smell. Some of the Cable operators had served in the Crimean War and one of them had a Crimean medal which, whenever he met Dr. Hamel, he took good care to have displayed prominently on his coat. The Doctor was also the subject of a Valentine rhyme called "The Russian Spy" circulated on the island, linking his name with that of Miss Maria FitzGerald of Reenglass.

Some importance must have been placed on Dr. Hamel's presence, because when the Directors of the Company met at the Hotel and "found old Hamel pretending to be asleep", they asked help from Lecky Senior and then the "Board meetings were in our dining room and the table they sat at was a circular slab of slate".

On the evening of Friday 7th August the squadron sailed, and the Niagara commenced paying out the cable very slowly. Unfortunately, after such a marvellous beginning, on the evening of Tuesday, the 11th, all signals from the cable suddenly ceased. The cable had broken in 2000 fathoms of water, when about 330 nautical miles from Valentia. There were various technical difficulties to be overcome before a new cable could be made and laid. To quote John Lecky again:

> After the ships went away we had profound calm for a year. We heard of the new attempts being arranged and of the terrible storm the Agamemnon got into in the Atlantic, when she and the cable were so nearly lost. No visitors on the island, the FitzGeralds away, Father in London.

The cable may have broken but Valentia was already on the world map of communications.

It was not until 1865 that a working cable was finally laid, landing again at Foilhomurrum with great ceremony; people waited for days hoping for a glimpse of the "Great Eastern", the largest ship in the world at the time, which had been especially adapted to take the entire length of cable.

A newspaper account of the time reported that:

> They came from the mainland across Portmagee, or flocked in all kinds of boats from points along the coast, dressed in their best,

and inclined to make the most of their holiday, and a few yachts came from Cork and Bantry with less rustic visitors. Tents were soon improvised by the aid of sails, some cloths of canvas, and oars and boathooks, inside which bucolic refreshment could be obtained. Mighty pots of potatoes seethed over peat fires outside, and the reek from within came forth strongly suggestive of whiskey and bacon....nor was music wanting. The fiddler and the piper had found out the island and the festive spot, and seated on a bank, played planxty and jig to a couple or two in the very limited circle formed in the soft earth by plastic feet or ponderous shoemasonry, around which, sitting and standing, was a dense crowd of spell-bound, delighted spectators... the bright groupings of colour formed on the cliffs and on the waters by the red, scarlet, and green shawls of the women and girls, lighted up the scene wonderfully.

In his speech to the people assembled outside the Instrument Room, the Knight of Kerry quoted the first commercial message sent on the new cable "Glory to God in the highest, on earth peace, good will to men" and called for three cheers for Sir Robert Peel, who was among those present. The same message was sent by Queen Victoria to the American President.

By now the Cable Company, which in 1866 became the Anglo-American Company, was well established on Valentia. J. May was Superintendent, T. Brown and W. Crocker, Assistant Electricians, and G. Stevenson, E. George, and H. Fisher, the Instrument Clerks. A temporary telegraph station had been built on the cliff, a wooden building, "with a passage from end to end, with rooms for living and sleeping in to the right and left, and an instrument room at the far extremity. Outside, the wires were carried on posts in the ordinary way to the station at Knightstown, where they were conveyed to Killarney. The telegraphic staff and operators were lodged in primitive apartments like the sections of a Crimea hut". The large wooden building was later to form part of the hospital on the island.

In the very beginning, two men were required to record every message. One had to observe a moving needle and estimate what letter it represented. He called this out to the second man who recorded it. This primitive and laborious method was soon improved on, but the men had to be able to write rapidly and legibly. Dermot Ring remembers being told that his grandfather could write 40 words per minute. This was in longhand, writing easily and crossing all his t's and dotting all his i's. Typewriters were not used for some years as the early models were clumsy and slow.

In the beginning, the real skill was in transmitting and receiving but after World War I the technical skills became more important.

Richard Lovett, who visited the Station some time in the 1880s, left a very good account of what went on there. At that time, the Company had three cables, one of which was in direct communication with Emden in North Germany, by which continental messages were sent direct via Newfoundland and Cape Breton to New York. To quote Richard Lovett:

> The instruments occupy two rooms. In one, the operators are engaged with the Emden Cable, some transmitting messages to America; others to various parts of the continent via Emden. The messages are expressed in all languages and in various ciphers. As the operator reads the message, which is being spelled out by the instrument, he transmits it to Newfoundland and this is so

promptly done that the first half of the message is across the ocean before the other has left Germany. In the second room Stock Exchange work, press messages and private telegrams are coming and going. Four operators were hard at work on the Stock Exchange messages, all in cipher. 3,000 messages passed through in 24 hours. The Superintendent stated that a New York broker is apt to grow impatient if he cannot get a message through to London and a reply in the course of a few minutes".

The station was manned 24 hours a day, 365 days a year, necessitating staff who worked on shifts. The tariff for telegraph messages was reduced from £20 per 20 word message in 1866 to 6d per word in 1889 with consequent increase in the use of telegrams for business, personal and newspaper purposes.

The impact of additional permanent Cable Staff was felt on the island from the very beginning. The cost of feeding the clerks and the visitors helped the island economy.

The next important step was the construction of the spacious station at Knightstown designed by Thomas N. Deane, a Dublin architect, and built in 1868. Its construction and that of the first block of houses gave local employment. Even before the wings were added the administration building was spacious and included a carpenter's shop, coal store, painter's shop, engine room, weighbridge, and a store for cables, ropes etc.. There was also a battery room, mechanic's room, kitchen, station electricians room, cable room, cable test room, canteen and rest room, office and Superintendent's office.

The Cable Station.

The first Supervisor was James Graves and he remained in charge from 1865 to 1909. The Graves family and the Mackey family were, between them, to be represented on the Cable Staff at Valentia from the beginning to the end. James Graves was born in Chesterton, near Cambridge, England in 1833. Before coming to Valentia he had varied experience, as a teacher, a clerk with the Electric Telegraph Company, in the Jersey office of the Channel Islands Telegraphic Company and then as submarine electrician on the "Monarch". Finally, he joined the Telegraph Construction and Maintenance Co., who had the task of testing the new Atlantic Cable which was being manufactured. In 1865 he came to Valentia to train and take charge of the staff at Foilhomurrum for the same Company and then joined the Anglo-American Co. as Superintendent at Valentia.

By 1873 there were five Cable clerks, five Cable writers, three Cable checkers, seven land clerks, and two land checkers. Three years later the Cable clerks had increased to 14. In the early days the staff were mostly English, often having trained as Telegraph clerks with the Post Office. Tradition on the island is that very many came from Cornwall.

The domestic staff were islanders from the beginning if we are to judge by their names....Bridget Roche, kitchen maid, Norah Shaw, Mary

Spillane, and Kate Bourke. Jeremiah Ring, from near Kenmare, started as a Morse clerk in 1875, after a spell with the Post Office in Cork. Tim Ring, his son, began as a check clerk in 1899. In 1883 Thomas O'Connell, who seems to have been a clerk, had his services dispensed with; he was too fond of drink and careless at his work. Thomas O'Donoghue was an "Emden Clerk" in 1897 and a Cable clerk in 1901.

The O'Sullivan family - a typical Cable family c. 1900.

By this time the number of Irish-born staff was quite high if we are to judge by those shown in the Census. Second generation Cable Staff were from families like the Mackeys; John, son of Robert R. Mackey, was an operator aged 19; Timothy Ring aged 16; Charles and Arthur Graves sons of Arthur James Graves; Arthur Scaife; Edmond and Maurice O'Sullivan; Frederick Hearnden and Bertie Hardy all returned on the Census that they were Irish born. The Mess, the residence for unmarried officers, had names like Patrick O'Driscoll and Timothy Cremin; the domestic staff were all Irish-- Elizabeth Jolley, the housekeeper, Bridget McCarthy, the cook, and Norah McCarthy, the parlourmaid.

Because of the presence of the Station on Valentia, islanders were able to obtain employment in Cable Services all over the world. Kerry children could boast of relations in New York or Boston but islanders had cousins in Newfoundland, Vigo in Spain, in the Azores and in Africa. The European traffic manager of Western Union Head Office in London was a Valentia man, Willie Smith; the Superintendent in Penzance in Cornwall was a Coughlan from the island, and in Heart's Content in Newfoundland, his opposite number was a Mackey, one of the family connected with the Cable Service from its early days. Another Mackey, George, was boss in Fayal Azores and with him went Edward and George Johnson, Bob Mackey, and Patie Cremin. Dan Sullivan went to Delago Bay and was later made Coast Superintendent of all African stations. Thomas Sullivan went to Cape Verde, Michael FitzGerald to Galveston and Maurice Keating was in charge in Vigo, Spain. Others went to New York. At one time, the Chief Electrician on the Cable Ship "Lord Kelvin" was a Donoghue from Valentia. He made his home in Halifax, Nova Scotia, which was the home port of the "Lord Kelvin". He was a good example of the background of Cable families, because his father had at one time been Superintendent in Penzance, in Cornwall.

Sir Robert Peel addressing the crowd at the official opening of the Trans-Atlantic Cable.

The world's fastest operator was Joseph C. Smith from Valentia. Though they did so well in other areas, no islander ever became head of the Valentia Station. This may have been company policy, as a local man would have had too many connections to contend with. Several Superintendents were from Newfoundland, like Boss Richards and Bateman; Edmonds, Joe Liddicoat, Gus Longland and Jimmy Dennis were all Cornish.

Cable Staff at the turn of the Century.

Probably the man with the longest service was Patrick O'Driscoll who started in 1872 aged 16 and retired after 60 years service in 1932.

The greatest number of staff in Valentia were during World War I; soldiers were also stationed on the island to protect the station. This was the period of greatest prosperity on the island in the opinion of John O'Donoghue, now retired from farming and a keen observer of island affairs.

After World War I staff levels were reduced and when the State was set up a number of the English-born staff left.

The staff book for 1921 lists a total of 242 staff, many taken on as students. The 1922 book has some interesting entries -- William J. Hooper, who was washed off the rocks at the Lighthouse and drowned;

Arthur Burwell, who died of typhoid; another entry lists one dismissed for errors and one for drink. By 1922 the number employed had dropped to about 120 and from this on the numbers declined as competition from other lines and technical advances reduced the manpower. The Anglo-American Company was taken over by Western Union in 1911 and closed finally in 1966.

Apart from "graphers", the name given locally to the operators, the ancillary staff included carpenters, electricians, plumbers, painters, janitors and gardeners. In 1901 the instrument maker was James Mair, who was Scottish. These were all highly regarded and the Head Men were always addressed as "Mister". Services provided by the maintenance men were excellent. The rubbish was taken away, the drains cleaned and the services of the maintenance staff were available to the families as well as on the Station.

The Cable Staff had excellent houses, which were rent free; the houses were newly painted and papered for each new occupant; they had running water and electricity when such luxuries were unknown in rural Ireland. Every house had a maid and sometimes two. Dermot Ring, who grew up in one of the Station houses and who later worked in the company, remembers that the maids were treated like one of the family in the 1930s and were sometimes even related to them. Their last girl was paid 25/- per calendar month, a very good wage in those days. She ate in the kitchen with the family, but his father only joined them for his dinner; he had his breakfast and tea in the diningroom. In the previous generation the grandfather, old Jerry Ring, never entered the kitchen at all; he had all his meals served up to him in the diningroom, as did most of his contemporaries on the Station.

By 1885, the Station a library of 800 volumes of text books of all kinds and light reading in the shape of novels; periodicals supplied included *Telegraphist, Electrician, Engineering Mechanic, Knowledge, Graphic, Illustrated London News, Punch* and *The Times* daily. There was a full size billiard table and a large boat safe enough for picnics but too heavy for a small crew; this was supplemented by a small fleet of punts (row-boats) and out-riggers, the private property of the staff. Wags were very popular round the turn of the century. By 1930 the out-board engine had taken over. Sailing and regattas were very much part of island life. Women in general did not crew boats but were otherwise very much involved. In an era before motor cars, being on an island was not considered such a social disadvantage; every family had a boat and sometimes two.

The "Mess" at the Station was used for dances on special occasions like New Year's Night. It was also the scene of billiards tournaments and "Smokers", a kind of male get-together, where resources were pooled to buy the alcohol; a piano in the billiard room provided music for the music session and cards, mainly solo, were also played.

Even in the beginning "graphers" had sick pay for a period not exceeding one month and half pay for the second month, something that must have been unusual for any employees in 1871. If employed in Ireland, for not less than one year, each officer was entitled to a free passage home at the expiration of his service. The Station had its own doctor. According to the"*Telegrapher*" of 1885, "Many of the clerks who have been sent here from England have in a short time, had their health greatly improved, owing to their regular living and the fresh air always at their service".

Because of their isolation, the first English staff serving on Valentia were paid a "hardship allowance"!

The Station had hard and soft tennis courts. There were tennis parties on the courts in front of the staff houses. To quote the late Robbie Graves: "Not alone were matches played against Waterville and Cahirciveen but tournaments were organised for members and final days brought competitors arrayed in white flannels and ladies dressed in their summer best provided tea and cakes". The Royal Hotel had two tennis courts and the game was also played in the grounds of two island private houses, so there were many places to practise.

A cricket team was also formed and the company was willing to pay rent for a field to have a permanent pitch, though in the early years none suitable could be found. Cricket was later played in the sportsfield in the village. When a number of the staff transferred to Waterville on the setting up of the Station there, fears were expressed that the Valentia Station would not be able to field a full team. Doreen Kelliher, nee O'Sullivan, remembers that the Cable Eleven played a match against the Knight of Kerry's team and other matches against Waterville and Tralee. In this century the sportsfield just beyond the Cable houses was used for a variety of games.

Football was another form of sport and three different games were played.. rugby, soccer and Gaelic, this last being the sport of the native islanders rather than the Cable Staff. According to Doreen Kelliher, who grew up in the Cable Station, where her father was the Supervisor, girls played rugby with the boys in the sportsfield.

Soccer was particularly popular during the 1914-18 War and in the early 1920s when a large number of young men arrived from London and Penzance. They brought their soccer skills with them to play against Waterville and Ballinskelligs Cable Stations and the crew from a British destroyer, which for some years harboured in Valentia. The sportsfield between the Cable houses and the corner of Bachelor's Road saw many keenly fought games but when a strong westerly gale was blowing, an injudicious high kick could soar the ball into the sea where it had to be rescued by boat.

Valentia Theatrical group, in Dublin 1911.

The Cable Station had its own magazine, *"Fun at V. A. ",* mostly relating to events on the Station but including amusing poems, lampoons and stories.

Cable wives must have had some very advanced views because the island actually had a branch of the women's Suffragette Movement, whose chairwoman was Mrs Ring. There was also a branch of the Women's National Health Association, and one member, a Mrs O'Sullivan, was important enough to have her picture included in the *Journal* in 1911. The Association had been set up by Lady Aberdeen, wife of the Viceroy, the King's representative in Ireland. Lady Aberdeen visited the island in 1910.

The visit of the Association's travelling health caravan is remembered by a few old people. Lectures were given and slides shown to help people to combat tuberculosis. Years later, Brother Peadar Lynch recalled that the first time he ever saw moving pictures was when the health caravan visited the island. The FitzGeralds were also involved in the Association.

Supplies were never a problem. The village of Knightstown had excellent shops. After the railway came to Reenard, shopping in Cahirciveen was relatively easy, after one had crossed the ferry. A man came once a month from Tralee to take orders from one of the major shops there and at Christmas hampers were ordered from Harrods or some of the other London stores. According to local stories, a man who couldn't get work in the Cable Station in Valentia, went to look for a job in the London Cable offices but ended up in Harrods. He saw the opportunity to extend business by supplying Christmas hampers to the Cable Station on Valentia and perhaps the stations in Ballinskelligs and Waterville.

The island could boast that it had two golf courses. The course above Glanleam, near where the granite Celtic Cross stands, extended from Dohilla Road to the Lighthouse and back to Glanleam. Membership was five shillings per annum. The course had a hut for changing and it even had a primitive toilet. Members walked or cycled to play.

The second golf course was in "Daly's Field" and it also had a primitive pavilion. It closed some time in the 1920s, presumably when the numbers of the Cable Staff dropped.

Handball was also played in the Slate Yard, where there was a suitable gable end on a large store house. A more leisurely game was quoits (locally pronounced kwates), which was similar to the game of bowls but flat faced stones were used instead of woods and the "Jacks" were large stones placed about 20 or 30 feet apart.

There were afternoon tea parties and card games and most important, musical evenings. The participants may not all have come from the Cable Station as there was much inter-marrying with local girls, especially after local men were taken on. A photo taken of the Valentia Island Company at the Village Hall Entertainments during the Ui Breasil Exhibition in Dublin in 1911 shows how elegant the women were. That such a small island could produce so many Feis Ceol winners shows how much talent was available and the contestants were able to travel to Mitchelstown, Sligo and London to participate.

The late Robbie Graves remembered that before World War I dances were held in the Fisherman's Hall or St. Derarca's Hall. Dancing of the English type was popular in the Fisherman's Hall, music being provided by talented musicians from the Cable Staff. Lancers, mazurkas, the Boston-two-step, the Valetta and the old time waltz all went on into the late hours of Saturday night and successful and amusing fancy dress parties were also organised. As well as accomplished pianists, the Cable Station boasted violinists, flautists, and mandolin players.

When the Cable Ships were in the harbour, dances were held in the Mess and a return dance on board ship. This was a very elaborate affair with excellent food served by stewards in white jackets and gloves.

St.Derarca's Hall was the Catholic parish hall in Knightstown and it had a more Irish and Gaelic tradition. Its entertainments were on Sunday nights during which Kerry Sets were danced to the music provided by expert players on melodeon and fiddle. The island had a blind piper at this period, Michael O'Brien. The island also had a talented composer, Griselda O'Sullivan, whose Anglo-American Gavotte was published.

The island's Masonic Lodge (No. 130 Star of the West) was supported mainly by the Cable Staff. It had been founded in 1880 by Captain Needham, the Trinity College agent, and its members included the Knight of Kerry, Sir Maurice FitzGerald, James Butler, a landlord on the mainland, and John E. Cullum, the Superintendent of the Observatory. The bulk of the members were Cable Staff, though some of them may have served in stations on the mainland, like David Main, who was on the staff in Ballinskelligs.

A grouping of Engineroom staff. From L to R: J. O'Connell, T. Grandfield, T. Smith, T. O'Leary, T. Smith Snr., Unknown, M. Sugrue.

Due mainly to the influence of Sir Maurice FitzGerald, the Duke of Connaught, Queen Victoria's son, became the patron of the Valentia Lodge and two years after its foundation the Lodge presented the Duke with a "very beautifully illuminated address".

More important than all the Cable Service amenities were the salaries. All station employees were well paid. It is not easy to compare rates of pay with today, but a general rule was that an established "grapher" had the pay of a bank manager, a very good house, cheap living and many amenities like electricity and running water. The other staff, the electricians and the technicians as well as the painters, carpenters and maintenance staff, were all considered to be well paid, and they worked all the time and were sure of their money. £250 per annum was paid to J.H. Carson, a Cable clerk's starting salary in 1866; five years later he went to London as Superintendent. James Graves, the Valentia Superintendent, earned £700 per year in 1896 and W. Hearnden, Assistant Superintendent earned £425 in 1902. F.W. Hearnden earned £48 as a Junior Clerk in 1894 and £144 as a clerk in 1902. Supernumeraries in 1913 started at £36 per annum but they were all very young. Arthur Scaife and Arthur Graves were only 16 in 1901.

There were certain disadvantages. Valentia was an island and a remote one at that. "That devil of a ferry" made life very difficult and if the weather was stormy you might not get off the island at all. After the railway came to Reenard, travel was easier. Once you got off the island, you could get to anywhere on the railway with relative ease. You could even go by train to Cahirciveen for shopping, something not available to the staffs of the Cable Stations in Waterville or Ballinskelligs.

Hours of work were governed by the fact that a 24- hour service had to be maintained. In the 1920s there were three shifts per day, 6a.m.-2p.m., 2p.m.-10 p.m., and 10p.m.-6a.m., the night shift. On Sunday 11th January 1920 there were 42 men on the first of these shifts, 23 on the second and 20 on the third.

Shift work always produced difficulties both at work and at home. In 1885 Arthur Rhodes resigned because he could not conscientiously perform Sunday duty.

All staff members had to sign a secrecy agreement that they would not divulge any information that passed through their hands. At least one man, James Keneilly, was dismissed for infringing Rule 2, the secrecy rule. Whether the operators were able to prosper personally from any information passing through their hands was another matter. It was generally believed by outsiders, like local bank clerks, that Cable Staff made money on the Stock Exchange but this was heresay or perhaps envy.

Children seeking secondary education had to be sent to boarding school, but this was the norm unless one lived in major towns. The Scaife girls went to the Ursuline Convent in Waterford, where the other boarders came from all over Ireland. Later, in the 1920s Evelyn Jerrem, daughter of the Supervisor, went to Loreto Convent in Rathfarnham. Others went to Sion Hill Convent in Dublin and the non-Catholic girls went to La Rochelle in Cork.

Church of Ireland boys went to Bishop Foy's in Waterford or to Kilkenny College. Most of the Catholic boys went to the Christian Brothers in Cahirciveen, though a few went to the Diocesan College in Killarney or to Rockwell College in County Tipperary.

Living in such a small community and on an island must have resulted in some personality clashes. There was the additional difficulty of living with all the people who worked with you as well as having a Resident Superintendent on the spot. This style of life was common to all Cable Stations and Valentia was considered easier in some ways than Heart's Content in Newfoundland. The winter was more severe there and there was no village and no farming hinterland. At least one operator, Henry Ring Crocker, left Heart's Content in 1868 because he could not stand the climate.

Considering the varied backgrounds and religions of the staff, Catholics, Church of Ireland, Church of England, United Methodist, Presbyterian, and Congregationalist, Valentia Station seems to have had very little friction. Doreen Kelliher considers that Ecumenism was in practice there long before the word was invented.

There were never enough staff houses to accommodate everybody and newcomers had to make do with cottages and whatever they could get round the island. A few substantial houses, like Eden Villa, could also be rented. Not all the "graphers" wanted accommodation in the Cable Houses. Some of those from the island, who had family homes, opted to live away from the Station. The Cable Houses were available only to serving staff until the 1930s so the difficulty of obtaining accommodation on retirement meant the "company houses were a bind".

Life on the Cable Station has been described as "Outpost of Empire" style. A grapher's life might be considered easy by a man with a small farm or by a fisherman but there was always the difficulty of keeping up the speed of sending messages and the unsocial hours of shift work. The physical dexterity to send messages at speed was essential and men were constantly seen exercising their fingers to keep them supple. Any damage to the hands could be very serious and the threat of rheumatism or arthritis was always there.

The Station had pioneers in new technology; there were instances of new inventions being suppressed and of staff leaving because they did not get recognition for their discoveries.

Dermot Ring summed up the situation: "You might be a big man walking about the village in your waistcoat and watch-chain but back in the Cable Station be called in to Graves' office for a minor transmission or receiving error. If this was a Stock Exchange transaction, it could have enormous consequences. The fact that you were trustworthy sending messages between Heads of State didn't save you from the repercussions if mistakes were made".

From the 1930s onwards the possibility that the Station would be closed down was also very real and until that period company houses had to be surrendered on retirement. What is quoted today about the men of the Cable Service is probably fair comment: "They were no better educated or more clever than anyone else but they were better paid".

The Cable ship Lord Kelvin on her last visit to Valentia in 1963.

Chapter Five
Landlords, Tenants and
Emigration.

Stories about the Knights and their tenants abound in Valentia folklore but it is difficult after so many years to be sure to which Knight the incidents relate.

Peter FitzGerald "reigned" for almost 30 years, all of which were spent on Valentia. A resident improving landlord, he was involved in all the island's activities but he is remembered most for his dealings with his tenants.

Because Ireland had no Industrial Revolution and very few known minerals, land remained the main source of wealth. To quote Trench, a landlord in Carrickmacross, Co. Monaghan, writing to Peter FitzGerald.... "competition for land in Ireland has been a furore.... Temptations to landlords to rackrent were almost bewildering". Peter FitzGerald described one incident on the Island. "A little girl of mine, of about 5 or 6 years of age, was playing on the lawn before my door, when a suitor for a farm watched his opportunity and placed in her small fist a dirty roll of greasy National Bank notes. It was intended to reach head-quarters in the hope of obtaining what is technically called "preference for a farm".

Yet, the demand for land cannot have been as great on Valentia as in other areas because in the 1860s, when the above correspondence took place, the Slate Quarry was flourishing.

The best remembered account of the Knights' dealings with their tenants is the removal of the Coarhabeg and Ballyhearny tenants to new farms at the foot of Bray Mountain.

According to Robert FitzGerald, son of Peter, the 19th Knight, who gave evidence to the Congested Districts Board in 1908, his father had done much to relieve congestion. About 1866 there were a number of holdings at Coarhabeg held jointly by two or more tenants. To improve the position, Peter fenced in a considerable portion of land in his possession, at the foot of Bray Mountain, about a quarter of a mile to a mile from the original holdings; he built substantial houses thereon, and insisted on lots being drawn as to which of the co-tenants should be migrated. As far as possible the remaining holdings were re-arranged. There was more land on the new holdings but it was poorer; the houses were very good, better than the former ones. It would appear from Robert FitzGerald's evidence that tenants were also brought from two townlands near Dingle and placed in one farm in Coarhabeg.

The number of tenants involved in the removal from Coarhabeg was small, so this re-arrangement was of less importance than the transfer of the Ballyhearny tenants to Bray. The Ballyhearny lands had been leased to the O'Connell family of Derrynane. When the lease expired in 1873 the lands were let in small patchwork fields, an example of the lowest type of "rundale". The worst was the holding of Michael Casey, which was only 20 perches wide and one mile and 14 perches long, extending from the sea at one end to the top of the mountain at the other.

Peter FitzGerald claimed that as the tenants in Ballyhearny were not his and that as the land had been subdivided when this was in contravention to the terms of the lease, he had no obligation to the tenants, but he was prepared to do his best for them. He wrote: "I must have laid out on a given area of land, a larger amount than has been spent by the wealthiest and most liberal English landlord." He also claimed that if all the land on the island was divided between the existing tenants and the landless cottiers, nobody could make a decent living.

Robert FitzGerald, Peter's son, later held that from the landlord's point of view this re-arrangement was not a profitable transaction. Although a new house had been built for almost every tenant in the townland and much fencing had been done, the total rent had dropped from £266 in 1873 to £208, at the time of his evidence.

So much for the landlords version of the affair. Local lore tells that others apart from the co-tenants were told to go and that some of the re-arranged holdings were given to the Knight's favourites. "Either both the sub-dividing parties must leave the lands, or they must settle amongst themselves who shall go" is also remembered. In all 26 tenants from

Ballyhearny were forced to go. Because these were reluctant to move, the parish priest gave a very stirring sermon from the pulpit at Sunday Mass in Chapeltown. He asked the people "Is it Paris you want?" The area along the road at the foot of Bray Mountain was always called "Paris" after that until recent years when so many of the old properties were bought by non-nationals that some local wags re-named it "Little Berlin".

"Paris", Valentia.

The regular laid-out fields at the foot of Bray Mountain, with the line of slated houses along the road, can still be seen today.

Other tenants were moved to an area between bog and cliff at Imlagh, exposed to every gale that blows in from Culloo.

Some of the migrants survived in the new farms but others emigrated. Perhaps the best account of the scheme is given by the late Liam McGabhann, the celebrated journalist, who grew up on the island: "It broke many a spade and many a man". If the land had been reclaimed for some years before the migrants were moved in to "Paris" and if the rents had been lower, it might have been a more feasible project. It must have been very hard for the tenant to appreciate a development for the general good, especially if he was the one who had to go.

Now, only little over a hundred years later, it is difficult to imagine that landlords were so powerful and that tenants had neither fair rent, fixity of tenure nor free sale, the "Three F's" later demanded by the Land League.

Sometimes the stories that have survived relate to the FitzGerald wives. One man was told off by Lady FitzGerald when another child was born into a large family who lived in poverty. The father was quick to remind Her Ladyship that "there was no poverty under the blanket".

As early as 1814 Thomas Radcliff reported that the Knight of Kerry had built many comfortable farm houses, both two-storied and slated. The O'Donoghue farm-house at Feaghmaan is believed to be over 200 years old and there are numerous similar farmhouses scattered all over the island. It was the cottiers or landless men who lived in very bad houses. The FitzGerald children left a graphic description of one such house. Mary wrote to her father in July 1851: "We went to see a poor old woman today. Her cabin on the outside was about 3 yards long and 2 broad. There was a door-way in which Bessie could stand upright and no window. She had no bed and hardly any covering; she must have been cold at night for there was no door."

Sir Peter FitzGerald seems to have been more popular with his tenants than his son, Sir Maurice. Because Maurice was absent from the island when he inherited and for some years afterwards, the estate was administered by his brother, Robert, referred to by the islanders derisively as "Roibeardín", or little Robert.

Robert was also the agent for the Trent Stoughton property on the mainland and at later stage for the Trinity College estates. He seems to have been unpopular and was involved in several court cases including that of Nano O'Connor, where the tenant claimed that she was being ejected even though she owed no arrears. This was the period of the Land War and the time when all over Ireland there were confrontations between landlord and tenant. The Valentia tenants claimed that at the previous general election the Nationalist candidate severely criticised the attitude adopted by the Knight towards his tenants. After this, according to the Cork Examiner of March 30th 1894, "accidently or otherwise, the landlord omitted to pay the rates for such tenants as were rated under £4 until the prescribed time for doing so had elapsed." As many of the islanders had rateable valuations of less than £4, they were then disfranchised.

In December 1891, two bailiffs came from Tralee to seize the cattle of tenants who were unable to pay the year's rent due to the landlord.

The bailiffs, protected by the Valentia police, proceeded to the townland of Ballyhearny and seized five cows belonging to John Murphy and five belonging to William Casey, who owed £13 and £14 rent respectively. They then proceeded to Feaghmaan and seized the cattle of a poor widow named Johanna O'Connell and cattle belonging to John O'Donoghue for rents of £14 and £23.13s.0d. Each of the tenants borrowed the rent from neighbours and redeemed the cattle. When the bailiffs went on to Coarhabeg they found nothing to seize -- the tenant had removed all stock, having been warned of the approach of the bailiffs.

According to Brother Peadar Lynch, who probably knew more of the island's local history than anyone else, it was generally believed on the island that as it was unusual to make a seizure for a single year's rent, the Knight was getting his own back on the tenants because the committee of the Valentia Dispensary had voted against his nominee, Dr. Price, for the position of Medical Officer to the Dispensary.

To quote Brother Peadar Lynch again: "With the backing of the National Land League, of which there was a vigorous branch in the island, the tenants demanded in 1885, a rent reduction of thirty per cent. The Knight, or "Roibeardin" acting for him, refused and issued ejectment notices, but then thought better of it, and offered a reduction of 25%, which the tenants accepted."

Rents were reduced by the Land Courts but the tenants considered they were victimised if they belonged to the Land League or applied to the Land Courts. Timothy O'Driscoll of Feaghmaan, who was prominent in the Land League Movement, claimed that he was victimised for making public the condition of the Valentia tenants. As a result he was compelled to pay his November rent on the day it was due, instead of in March of the following year.

The final stage of Maurice FitzGerald's dealings with his tenants began in 1910 when negotiations commenced for the purchase of his estate and that of Trinity College by the Congested Districts Board. Maurice wrote that he was reluctant to sell because he had such good relations with his tenants but, if this was what they wanted, he would facilitate them. By this time Sir Maurice was elderly and had gone to live permanently on his lands in England. Most of the negotiations were conducted between his English agent, Col. Lockhart Ross, and the Tenant's Committee. The papers dealing with the sale, which are stored in the Land Commission, show that the Colonel was bitterly anti-Irish. According to the Congested Board's Inspector he "speaks of Irish matters and the management of Irish affairs and Irish men in the most contemptuous tone".

The purchase price which the tenants were to pay for their land was based on the reduction they could obtain on their existing rent. They looked for a greater reduction than the 5/- in the pound offered and a committee was set up to look after their interests. A further reduction, 6/- in the pound, was then offered but Ross specified that the offer was to hold only "until the post which leaves the island on Monday 11th April 1910". This offer was not accepted and the negotiations dragged on until 1913. One elderly man is remembered as saying that all he wanted in this life was "blian amhain eile", one more year, so that he could live to see the ownership of the land.

A sum of £215 was deducted from the value of the estate for evicted farms and the papers have references to evictions in the years before the sale. It is also remembered that there were very bad evictions on the Herbert estate before it was sold to the FitzGeralds.

Even those who were evicted were sometimes able to get the better of the Knight. A man evicted from Dohilla had a house built for him on a plot at Tragannane which was considered "no man's land". The quarry workers stole the slates from the quarry to provide a roof and much of the walls were made from slate as well. In tales of evictions the landlord's agent was usually remembered rather than the Knight.

Other memories of the Knight at this period include the Christmas party given to the schoolchildren, who got presents of mugs with pictures of the King and Queen. Milk from Glanleam was given free to the school and vegetables to the Hospital.

When World War I broke out, the Knight encouraged Valentia men to join the British army and promised "tenants who join will not be asked to pay rent". These were cottiers and the poorest, not farmers who would have already become owners of their land.

Compared with other parts of Ireland there were no wholesale evictions and no clearances. Confrontations with the law were minimal and there occurred nothing like the scale of agrarian trouble in County Tipperary which, at one period, had the highest rate of agrarian crime in Ireland. Certainly there were no attempts on the life of the landlord or his agent as happened on Lord Leitrim's estate or the lands at Glenveigh in Donegal.

No stories have survived about the tenants of the O'Connells or the Spotswoods who leased land from the Knights early in the last century and let it to tenants but tales of the conditions of Trinity College tenants have been handed on.

Captain Needham, Trinity College Agent, dressed in his regalia as a Mason.

55

All accounts of conditions on the College lands describe poverty and want. A survey published by Maurice Collice in 1845 stated "College property was a good example of a grossly overcrowded poverty-stricken estate of the period."

Later, Charles Russell, writing his "New Views on Ireland" in 1880, was even more condemnatory... "A more squalid tenantry than that of this rich corporation it is hardly possible to conceive". He also considered rents too high and there was a need for large scale drainage works.

Toler Garvey, a professional land agent of Birr, Co. Offaly, wrote that "it would be difficult to conceive anything more thoroughly barbarous than their dwellings or more miserable than their mode of living". Other descriptions were of "dens and hovels", these being the habitations of the "cabin holders" rather than those who held any sizeable amount of land.

Captain Needham, the first agent after the College took over the administration of the estate, was sometimes in disfavour with his employers. The Burser of the College complained that on Lord Lansdowne's estate there were little or no arrears of rent, unlike the Trinity estates. Needham asked the Manager of the Munster Bank in Cahirciveen if he knew of any College tenant who had made money from his farm. He forwarded the reply to the Burser that the lands "did not show much profit", but he added "it is wonderful how they scrape money together sometimes for fortunes for their daughters."

Butler, Needham's successor, was tougher in his dealings with the tenants and as a result received from the Board a gift of 50 guineas and £24 per year to pay a clerk. Prices for agricultural produce were very low when Butler took over and this was also the beginning of the Land League. Complaints were made by the Board of the College that so little rent was being collected. Butler was very quick to point out that he had collected £500, 1/3 of what was due but no other agent had got more than 1/5 of the usual rents.

As in their dealings with the Knight of Kerry, the islanders were able to get the better of the College agents. A Trinity tenant in Cool owed rent. He knew that there was an eviction order made against him by the agent and that he needed to watch out. One Fair Day in Cahirciveen, this tenant was driving a beast down the quay from the cattle boat, when he spied the bailiff looking to see who had cattle. He told a neighbour to sell the cow and doubled back home to Cool. About an hour later the bailiff knocked on the tenant's door. A child's voice told him to put in his finger and lift the latch. The Bailiff put in his finger and it was cut off by a hatchet. The voice said "Put in another finger now, my man". The agent did not chance it and the tenant's family remained in possession.

The College did make some improvements. In response to a request from Miss FitzGerald, the Board granted £50 towards the cost of a permanent building for the Hospital. Miss FitzGerald was at pains to point out that, in 1882, 18 patients out of 39 admitted to the Hospital were from the Trinity Estate and, in 1883, 16 out of 40. The widow and children of one of the Church of Ireland rector's, Rev. Mr. Sandiford, received £20 and the Kerry Protestant Orphan Society got £10 per annum.

Other improvements paid for by the College were £31 for a sand boat for tenants in Tinnies, forges at Cahir and Portmagee and £37.11.0. for a road and quay at Tinnies. They also gave loans at 5%, like that to Martin Driscoll at Tinnies for building his new house. In 1870 they gave £40 for a road at Cool.

The total rent from the Trinity College lands on the island was £531.7.6. in 1866 but only £502.2.9. was collected. The highest rent was £10. 5.4. paid by John Murphy in Cool East, but most amounts were only two or three pounds.

Emigration was part of everyday life on the island. Even after the Great Famine, when the population dropped steadily, only one son could make a decent living on any farm. The Quarry, when operating, and the fishing, would have absorbed some of the surplus. When the Cable Station was established it was also a source of employment. The island probably had better opportunities for non-farming employment than most rural areas but there was never enough for everybody.

People were emigrating to America even in the early 1800s. When the American, Arseneth Nicholson, visited Valentia just before the Great Famine, she met a man who had returned to the island having spent years in her native town in Vermont.

Another early emigrant was the Fenian leader in America, Colonel John James O'Connor, who left Caol (Chapeltown) as a child of three in 1844 with his family, settling first in Boston and later in Braintree Mass..

57

O'Connor returned to Ireland after service in the Federal Forces in the Civil War and led Kerry Fenians in the rising of 1867.

Peter FitzGerald certainly wished to encourage emigration as shown in drawings from his papers.

Trinity College was also keen to promote emigration and its records give some details of its involvement.

In 1880 a report by Toler Garvey suggested that some cottiers should be re-housed and the rest induced to remove off the estate. He proposed building 16 new cottages and that the vacated hovels should be immediately levelled "while the remaining 24 families should be induced to emigrate or remove elsewhere off the College lands by the offer of £5 to the tenant and £1 in addition for each child. A good many would go off the estate almost at once---where they go you need not enquire."

When James Butler took over from Captain Needham as agent, he wrote in 1884 that "there were about 40 in Valentia and Portmagee whose cabins were rented at 2/- to 5/- per annum, most of them have paid no rent for 4 or 5 years, many being little better than beggars." Butler suggested that one year's rent only should be accepted as if they were let run on too long "there would be the danger of their establishing a free-hold, the thing of all others to be guarded against".

Also that year, James Butler mentioned that he had attended a meeting of the Valentia and Portmagee Free Emigration Committee and that there were 29 families with an average of 8 persons wishing to go. In May 23 families (150 souls) from Portmagee and Valentia emigrated.

Other efforts of assisted emigration included the payment of £2 each to 24 tenants in July 1883.

What is best remembered in island folklore is the "Free Emigration" when the British Government undertook a large scheme, giving £5 per head for adults, half for children and £1 for infants. A condition of the scheme, which was administered by the Board of Guardians, who selected the eligible emigrants, was that the family should emigrate as a whole. It was found that money could be saved by arranging for ships to call at selected points on the coast apart from the normal ports. So it was that the Belgravia, 5,000 tons, of the Anchor Line, on her way from Liverpool, entered Valentia harbour in the late evening of Thursday, June 1st, 1883, and came to anchor beneath Glanleam, to take on board the following day more than 800 from the Barony of Iveragh, of whom a high proportion came from Valentia. The embarkation of the passengers was supervised by Captain Hutchinson from the ship and by Captain Sampson, Local Government Inspector; Major Spaight; Mr James Butler, chairman of the Cahirciveen Board of Guardians, and the Clerk of the Union, Mr. M. O'Driscoll. According to the *Cork Examiner*, the emigrants were all tidily dressed and presented a healthy appearance.

The shores of the harbour in Valentia and the adjoining mainland were crowded with friends and relatives, bidding adieu to the emigrants. "In the crowd of over 5,000 assembled on the shore, not a single case of drunkenness was noticed nor tumult of any kind, and the sad work of sending off from the shores of Ireland of so many of her sons and daughters proceeded with a quietness benefiting the solemn occasion."

Being a steam screw-propelled vessel the Belgravia took only nine days to cross the Atlantic, a great improvement on the days of the sailing ships, so often known as "coffin ships". Even so, as the passengers travelled steerage, they must have been glad to reach New York.

Harrowing scenes of grief marked the departure of the Belgravia but this was not the end of the island's loss. On June 16th of the same year, many more emigrants bid farewell to kith and kin as they boarded the Furnessia, also of the Anchor Line.

For years afterwards islanders like Seamus (Jamsie) Lynch, formerly of Coarhamore, told how he was taken by the hand by his elder brother to view the giant ship, the Furnessia. Mrs Jerry O'Sullivan would recall to her children that a young couple, man and wife from Coarhabeg, called to her shop for provisions on their way to the emigrant ship. And especially the man's words to his wife "Teanam ort, a Nora. Is fada uainn an baile", (mind you, Nora, we are a long way from the town (of New York).

Perhaps the saddest memory was that of Patsy Lynch of Lotts, near Chapeltown. He was a boy of about 12 years, attending at Ballyhearny school in 1883. There were 220 on the rolls but on the day after the last ship, the Furnessia, sailed, there were only 56.

More recent emigration is recalled by Mrs Catherine O'Donoghue in Feaghmaan. She tells of a girl born in 1908, who emigrated when she was 17. She went by boat from Cobh, having stayed overnight. When she arrived in New York she was interviewed by the authorities on Ellis Island. She was met by an aunt who had never seen her. To overcome the difficulty of identification, the aunt had sent her a coat to Valentia with instructions to wear it so that she would be recognised.

Girls who had worked in Cable Station houses at this period were regarded as "trained" domestics on arrival in America and could command very good wages.

Islanders emigrated to New Zealand at two different periods, the children of the first emigrants bringing out their nieces and nephews in the next generation. Apart from those who emigrated to work in Cable Stations all over the world, most went to the United States.

Valentia Island peasants - taken from an article which appeared in the French periodical *A Travers le Monde* in August 1907.

Chapter Six
The Quarry.

In the first half of the nineteenth century, the great Slate Quarry at Geokaun was the largest single source of paid employment on Valentia. It gave the islanders "cash flow" and provided jobs for the sons and occasionally the daughters of the farmers, fishermen and landless labourers.

The Slate Quarry on Valentia was first opened in 1816 on the east slope of Geokaun on land which the Knight of Kerry, Maurice FitzGerald, leased from Trinity College. Conn O'Neill, living in Laharn, opened the first hole to the west of Carraig na Cuirte, on the far side of the mountain from the large opening visible today, and it was called "Poll ui Chuinn", Conn's hole, ever after.

The early working was on a small scale giving very little employment but already in 1821 Knightstown, with its slate yard and harbour was the scene of "Boats, ships, bustle and activity". The Irish Mining Company took over the Quarry in 1825 and began to expand it. The operation cannot have been too successful because the Mining Company pulled out and the Knight resumed control after six years.

The Knight used his money and his influence to promote the undertaking. He spent £16,000 on the works, a very large sum at that time. This money may have included the loan of £7,000 which the Knight obtained from the Commissioners of Public Works between 1831 and 1835. The Knight must have been very quick to look for assistance from the recently established Board, because his was the fourth loan given by them.

The Knight also used his contacts and influence to help sell the finished slate. The FitzGerald papers contain a copy of a letter to the Knight from the Duke of Wellington, who wrote:

You may rely upon it that I will go to Tooley Street to see the sample of your slate and I will read the ordinance report and if I can I will promote the interest of your quarries. I have a good deal of farm building of my own going on to which I will apply your slate if it answers the purpose.

The Knight was never slow to use his influence and in this case he succeeded, because the Duke's dairies at Stratfield Saye were shelved with Valentia slate.

Maurice FitzGerald obtained a second lease from Trinity College in 1839 for 21 years at a rent of five shillings sterling per year. At the last year of the 21 year lease, the College were to be paid one shilling sterling for every merchantable ton weight of slates or flags raised and FitzGerald was to spend £100 yearly on improvements.

In 1839 Maurice FitzGerald leased the Quarry to an English company, the Messrs Blackburn, who under the name of Valentia Flag Company operated it until 1877. They ploughed a further £40,000 into the extension and improvement of the works and enjoyed considerable success. An article in the *Dublin Builder* of 1st December 1863 considered that too much of the capital was spent on the machinery, mills etc. and not enough on the actual Quarry. The opening of the mine was said to be then 120 feet wide and in need of extension and there was ample room for the deposit of waste. This was probably the opening on the west side, where the Grotto is today.

In the 1860s the Quarry, and therefore the island, prospered. Decline set in during the 1870s due to competition from soft Welsh slabs and cheap Welsh and American roofing slates. The Valentia Flag Company must have been finding the going difficult because it handed the Quarry back to the Knight. Sir Peter FitzGerald was an old man at this stage and already in failing health, so he was unable to repeat the rescue operation conducted by his father in 1831 and after six or seven years the Quarry closed. Conditions throughout Kerry, and all the western seaboard, were desperate in the 1880s and 1890s and, after repeated demands, the industry was restarted around the turn of the century. The smaller opening to the west of the main Quarry seems to date from this period and it was here in 1911 that a rockfall took place which was responsible for the final closure of the works. No one was injured because the men had been called out to help save the Knight's harvest. Tradition on the island tells that the men's tools were buried under the fallen rock.

The slate was quarried in great blocks. They were first shifted out of their position by gunpowder and handwork, then lifted by a travelling crane, which was suspended from the roof of the quarry and put on wagons for carrying to the squaring-house, where they were placed under two sets of parallel saws and squared off. A set of blades for a frame saw was ordered by Peter FitzGerald in 1877, "41/2 x55 long and a set of buckles". He also ordered a small saw for cutting iron.

The squaring house was just outside the quarry face, a large house with sliding doors and a chimney 50 feet high, the remains of which are still to be seen. Here the rough ends and sides were sawn off and the blocks then brought down to the Slate Yard in the village of Knightstown, just behind the Royal Hotel. In the yard they were sawn by long strips of iron saws without teeth, worked backwards and forwards by machinery and attended to by sawyers constantly feeding the saws with fine flint gravel brought from Bridfort in England and a constant drip of water. The company had its own water supply.

The blocks were usually 14ft x 6ft for the London market but they could be up to 20ft long, and occasionally 30 ft. They cost at one stage 35/- to 55/- per ton according to the size of the slabs. About 150 ft of slab an inch thick went to a ton in size.

To get such huge blocks from the Quarry to the Slate Yard in Knightstown was a major undertaking. They went in horse-drawn carts but later a small railway on tracks, with an engine called "puffing Billy", brought the huge slabs down. The wagons at one stage are said to have worked on a pulley system; the wagons going down pulled those going up. There were also wagons drawn by horses, six stables being provided.

The Slate Yard was where the final work was done. All the very substantial buildings there were built of slate and the yard itself was slate paved, the remains being visible today. Even the window frames of some buildings were made of slate. The chimney in the Slate Yard is clearly visible in the Lawrence photo No. 4594 but only the base remains today.

The number of men working at the Quarry and in the Slate Yard in Knightstown varied. According to Lady Chatterton, who visited the island in 1839, there were "about one hundred"; the same number was quoted by Finlay Dun in 1881 but the greatest number must have been in the years of the Great Famine, we know from Maurice FitzGerald's correspondence with the British Government about the threatened famine, that 500 people were employed but the company were about to let off 200 of these. It appears that in very busy times both men and women worked in the mine and the Slate Yard but unfortunately we do not know what the women did.

When the mine opened in 1816, Welsh miners were brought over to show the local men how to work the mine. We know the name of one, John Jones, because when his wife gave birth to a daughter in 1827 she was christened in the Church of Ireland. The father, John Jones, gave his occupation as "Overseer of Slate Quarry". Presumably Thomas Shuel, the mason from Laharn, whose son Jeremiah was christened in 1828, also worked in the mine. Others were John Shuel of Tennies who gave "Nailor" as his occupation in 1833, as did Thomas Carter of Laharn. The Church of Ireland records show other foreign names like Joseph Admonston (1846) of Knightstown, a stone cutter, Vitus Merrick (1848), an engineer, and in 1874 another Jones who was also a Foreman in the Slate Quarry. In 1901 Evan William Evans was the Assistant Supervisor.

Even though the supervisors were Welsh during most of the period when the quarry was worked, the bulk of the workmen were local. In 1901, the Census lists John Murphy from Cool East as a farmer and quarryman; Patrick Reardon was a labourer and quarryman and John Connor a mason, all from Tinnies Lower East; in Ballyhearny West, Philip Sullivan was a sawyer and Michael O'Donoghue a quarryman; in Feaghmaan West, Patrick Donoghue was a "slate dresser". The greatest number of quarry workers lived in Dohilla, directly under the quarry itself. Peter Donoghue was a mason, John Shea and his son, also John, were quarrymen. Other names were John Neill and Cornelius Shea and Evan W. Evans, the foreman, who like his wife, Elizabeth, came from North Wales.

At the middle of the last century, the quarry foreman was Dan Jones. His father, "old Jones", weighed the slabs en route to the schooners and had a small office and platform-weighing machine, just outside the lower gate of the yard, close to the pier, where the schooners waited to be loaded.

The Welshmen associated with the Quarry were supervisors and technically qualified tradesmen, but the manager for the period of its greatest prosperity was an engineer named Bewicke Blackburn, who became quite famous as an inventor and whose daughter, Helen, became involved in the Suffragette movement and was the author of books on women's rights and the women's movement.

The Blackburns spent about 22 years on Valentia (1837-59 approx.) living first in the house off the Coombe Road, now O'Driscoll's farm, which they rented from the Knight and later at the substantial house on the front where the Allied Irish Bank sub-office is today. The Blackburn children were very friendly with the children of Peter FitzGerald and the FitzGerald papers contain correspondence about Hallow Eve parties and about collecting ferns. After he left Valentia, Blackburn kept in constant touch with the Knight of Kerry, mostly on matters relating to the Quarry. There is nothing to show why Blackburn pulled out of Valentia. Perhaps he thought he needed a wider market for his talents. He was the inventor of the "Blackburn Steam Car", a prototype of the motor-car and he patented improvements in velocipedes. In his later years he conducted a lively correspondence with Miss FitzGerald, advising her on what kind of bicycle to buy.

Blackburn was succeeded at the mines by Lecky, a Cork ship-builder, who was a Quaker. The Leckys lived in the Blackburn house on the front and Lecky's son left a description of their garden there; four acres, where they had a rifle range and where they grew the year's stock of potatoes, a small meadow for hay, greens, cauliflowers, celery, huge rhubarb and roots of all sorts, including artichokes. Their flowers included Arum Lillies. The Lecky interest in botany may have been started during their life on the island. Later it was to bring fame to a daughter, Susan Lecky. The Lecky children were very interested in boats and sailing and left the account that "our life was very peaceful; Father was in the Slate Yard all day or up in the Quarry." Lecky was also involved in the setting up of the Meteorological Station.

Slate was used for a variety of purposes. Roofing slate was produced in the 1860s for the local market, but Valentia slate was not considered ideal. It was too heavy and required very good support. Yet the British House of Commons at Westminister is said to be roofed with Valentia slate, something quite credible when one remembers all the correspondence with the Duke of Wellington. The Public Record Office in London had 25 miles of shelving made from Valentia Slate. Slate was produced for local markets in the 1860s and all the roofing slate was got from the waste of the large blocks. This was transported by small coasters to ports such as Dingle, Kenmare, Kilrush, Askeaton etc. Many of the islanders earned a living from this trade, an ancillary industry to the Quarry. The local trade in slates died in the 1870's.

The Harbour at Knightstown must have been a very busy place at this time. The schooners which brought the gravel to the island took away the slabs to London and where ever wanted. Lecky names the "Reaper", the "Gleaner"and the "Sir Charles Napier". Slabs went as far afield as South America where they were used in the construction of the San Salvador Railway.

Because it could be cut into very large slabs and was very strong, the slate was more suitable for flagging, fish slabs, dairy shelving, tables and billiard tables. The large slabs were also used for paving at Nottingham, Derby, Rugby and Leicester Railway Stations; in 1863 a large order was being prepared for Charing Cross, Blackfriers and Waterloo Stations. Portsmouth Barracks and the Race Stand at Brighton were customers, as well as Malting Houses in Bedfordshire and Hertfordshire breweries.

A look at the contents of Glanleam House which were sold in 1925 give some idea of what was made for the Knight's own use. There were tables, one two-tier, and fenders and most of the bedrooms had wash-stands with slate tops, including one which was octagonal, with a pillar and circular tray in the centre.

Outside were various slate tables, one being 4ft by 3 ft, and slate seats. Local labour was not always considered good enough for the Knight, because an Italian craftsman was brought in to work the classical wreaths on the slate fireplaces at Glanleam.

George Eugene Magnus, who had grown up in the Staffordshire potteries, where he learned the art of glazing, was to become a very important promoter of Valentia Slate. He acquired an interest in the works in 1838 and began to distribute its products from his Pimlico Slate Works. Between 1838 and the end of the century he created a "rage for slate in the homes of the nobility".

The Pimlico Slate Works specialised in "fine furniture with a practical application". Irene Cockroft, in an article titled "Used in the mansions of the nobility" in Country Life Magazine of February 1979, describes how steam power was used to cut, groove and mould slate into an infinite variety of polished ornamental items. To these were added slate mosaics and enamelled slate. Magnus used his knowledge of pottery glazing to develop a technique for applying decorative enamel to slate. So successful was he that Magnus Enamelled Slate won prizes at international exhibitions in 1851 and 1862. Magnus' really successful invention was his patented billiard table. It was composed entirely of slate, including the legs. This ensured that it did not become rickety under the weight of the top and would withstand termites in the tropics. These slate billiard tables were exported to Africa, India and even to Constantinople. The Duke of Wellington bought an enamelled slate table for his house, Stratfield Saye. One Royal order obviously begot more because, impressed by the Duke's table, Prince Albert, Queen Victoria's husband, ordered one to his own design for the new house at Osborne, on the Isle of Wight. It was enamelled to look like white marble.

Magnus Patent Billiard Table at Stratfield Saye. Photographed by kind permission of the 8th Duke of Wellington. Photographed by David Cockroft.

The Quarry was leased to George Magnus of the Enameling Company on 30th November 1877 and must have been operated by him or his son. Peter FitzGerald, then an old man, obviously kept an eye on the running of the mine because in the following year he wrote to Magnus that "the quarry road is in a dreadful state".

Among the entries in the "Building Manufactures" Section of the Dublin International Exhibition of 1865 was G.E. Magnus of 39 Up. Belgrave Pl., Pimlico, S.W. who offered chimney pieces and other works in enamelled slate. The Committee for the Machinery Section of the same exhibition included the Knight of Kerry. The Knight or the company must have been very keen to be well represented because another member of the Committee was Captain Needham, presumably the Trinity College agent.

Quarrying was a dangerous occupation. There was a rock fall in the winter of 1853 but it happened at night and no one was injured. Blackburn had presumed that the area had immunity from frost but the temperature remained below freezing for nearly a week following on a deluge of rain and this was considered the cause of the fall. At some period a crane swinging out a slab of slate broke and killed a man named Sugrue; according to local lore the slab that killed him was used as his tombstone. There are other stories of "two or three" people being killed and of miraculous escapes. One man saved himself by holding on to a bar when the ground gave way under him.

Some idea of the value of the sales from the Quarry can be got from the *Dublin Builder* magazine. In the 1840s exports were valued at £2,500 per annum and the flags were sold from 4d to 1s.3d per square foot. In 1860 2,000 tons of slabs were exported. According to an article in the *Dublin Builder*, £11,000 worth of slate for enamelling was ordered for one public building.

The miners' wages must have been an important part of the island economy at all stages. In 1837 they were paid 2s/6d per day, double that of the mainland workers. What is most remembered about wages of miners on the island is that in the 1880 period, when the mine was worked by the Knight, the miners were paid in yellow-meal instead of money. This seems incredible today but similar payments in meal were made in other Irish mines, especially in Tipperary after the Great Famine .

One man, a Carrick, protested about this method of payment, because he wanted cash to go to Killorglin to buy the heavy gutta-percha boots that all the miners wore. They walked to Killorglin and back to buy them, using 24 free hours of Sunday. Carrick is reputed to have written to the owner in England, presumably Magnus, and a man was sent to inspect the books, which were kept by O'Driscoll, the Knight's agent. These showed entries of "meal" after each worker. The late Jeremiah O'Leary, when discussing this incident, commented that perhaps the Knight was not entirely to blame, because if there was a total failure of the potato crop, money would have been no use if there was nothing to buy. Peter FitzGerald ordered Indian meal, whole and crushed, to be delivered to Valentia as early as December 1877.

The Carricks, who were stone masons, left some marvellous tombstones which can be seen in both the Protestant and Catholic cemeteries on the island. They were reputed to be prepared to carve a poor man's tombstone for half a pint of whiskey. They emigrated to America some time before the 1901 Census was taken... the name Carrick does not appear in it. They must have prospered in Brooklyn, however.

Valentia slate was used for tombstones outside the island. In nearby Ballinskelligs, the slate headstone to Patrick O'Sullivan of Ightercough, who died in 1841, was carved by John Millard of Valentia.

At some periods the miners were highly rated in the island's social scale. The novelist and journalist, Harriet Martineau, who visited in 1852, left a horrific description of the hovels of the landless peasants but was full of praise for the village of Knightstown and the slate works:

> At the little port there is a preventative station, a station of constabulary, a little inn renowned for its "fragrant cleanliness" and a large establishment of slate-works, in connection with the splendid quarries up on the hills. These slate works have been in operation 35 years, sustained by English capital, and conducted by English skill and care. The workpeople, however, are Irish, every man of them, except the overlooker, who is Welsh. ˙At present there are 120 men employed at the quarries and works; and the difference between this part of the population and the rest is so striking that the blind might be aware of it. It is not only that the men and boys, even those at the roughest work, can scarcely be called ragged at all; there is a look and tone of decent composure and independence about them which seems at once to set one down

among a company of well-paid English artisans. These people are all well paid and have sound training. Again, the proprietor of the slate works (Bewicke Blackburn) lives beside them. He and his lady are English; and they bring over English servants for their comfort. They also lose all these servants immediately. The best men at the works marry them, as surely as they see their neat ways and English industry."

The quarrymen were very skilled craftsmen. They knew exactly where to split the slate to get the maximum number of pieces and the least wastage. They were also reputed to be able to make their own blasting powder.

After the 1878 closure of the mine some of the workers emigrated but many went to work on the railway. When next you travel from Killorglin to Cahirciveen take a good look at the huge viaduct and wonder how many of Valentia's workers were involved in its stone work. The men left their island homes late on Sunday night to walk to the ferry to take them to Reenard Point, walked to Cahirciveen and then to the viaduct, carrying their parcels of home-made wholemeal bread which had to last them until the following Saturday night. Some sort of huts were provided for the men to sleep in but no provision seems to have been made for food.

The miners worked long hours and started the day early. It was a child's task before going to school to bring his father a bottle of hot tea wrapped in a sock to keep it warm. Unfortunately, very few other additional details of their working hours and conditions seem to have survived.

The best contemporary description of the mining operation is in an unsigned article entitled "Hope with a Slate Anchor" in Charles Dickens "*Household Words*" of 1853. At the mine there was

> .. an upper tramway, or precipice of slate, with a rough wall of slate behind it, in a vast chamber like the "great chamber of the Great Pyramid". Groups were clustered or half hidden in this enormous cavern; men with borers and mallets making holes for the blasting; men with wedges and mallets, splitting off great blocks; some on shelves high up overhead; some in cupboards far within; some in dark crevices in the mighty walls. Below, two

men with chains and hooks were fixing the hooks in crevices under the horizontal mass of slate. As the mass rose, they shifted the hooks further into the cracks, until the block broke off. The blocks were deposited in trucks at a lower stage by a man working a windless and block chain. The truck with the block on it was then drawn by a horse to the saw- mill where the block was again raised by machinery and placed in position for the saws. A single horse could draw a weight of five tons; the largest size actually weighed fifteen tons.

The noise of the mill was described as "horrid" ---- in kind as well as degree, so that the author of the article did not stay long near the mill. The noise in the Slate Yard at Knightstown was also reputed to be overwhelming but was not heard by the author as that day the works were stopped for repair of the machinery. A tour of the works revealed slabs of slate many feet long and from half an inch to three inches in thickness. They were stacked standing on edge leaning against each other. A boy was at work on one large piece, which had large round holes cut out of it, which was for the ridge of a house.

A visit to the proprietor's house, presumably Blackburn's, showed that all the steps and patios were made of slate, as well as umbrella and hat stands, a standard lamp, a handsome round table in the dining room, variegated somewhat like marble, with a moulded rim, well-turned stem and finished pedestal. The author also commented on the extensive use of slate at Glanleam, including a music-stand, a what-not, and a sofa table.

Anyone visiting Valentia should keep a look-out for all the items made from slate which still survive. The collection box for the hospital, set in a wall in the village, is probably the first item to meet the eye but watch out for paving stones, window frames in the Slate Yard, numerous stiles, the roof of a porch, walls of houses, the shores catching the water from the roof of the Church of Ireland, gutters on the road, garden seats, tables, shelves, grave stones, often decorated by the Carrick brothers, plaques on buildings and, of course, the modern sculpture created by Alan Hall of the Gallery Kitchen.

71

Chapter Seven
Fishing.

Fishing was an important part of the island economy, but it was an uncertain industry, depending on the supply and the market prices and most important of all, on the weather. After Dingle, Valentia was regarded as the largest fishing area in south-west Kerry.

The first account of fishing comes from Petty's Survey, about 1660, when he reported that about 160 "Saynes" fished off the coast for pilchards. He considered that Ireland was "commodious" for the trade to the new American world and should send butter, cheese, beef and fish to the settlements and plantations of America.

Smith, who wrote a later history of Kerry, considered in 1768 that the harbour of Valentia "is justly esteemed the best in these parts" and that the Channel between the island and Portmagee was wide enough for trading ships to sail through at any time of the tide.

The erection of a quay at the "Foot", the original name for Knightstown, by the Fishery Board in the early years of the nineteenth century, was an advantage to island fishermen. Part of the money, £705, came from the Government, £114 came from the Dublin Committee, and the Knight of Kerry gave £141.

Fishing was considerable at this period. Lewis, in his *Topographical Dictionary* in 1837, claimed that about 400 persons were exclusively occupied in the fishing on Valentia, in which 100 seine boats and 150 yawls were engaged. This must have meant 100 boats, including seines, as 100 seine-boats would have needed 1,400 men to crew them.

By 1871 the population of the island had declined and with it the fishing. According to Cusack's history published that year, the men who carried on the pre-famine fishing had died or emigrated and the few who remained had neither boats, nor nets, nor the capital to procure them.

Perhaps the availability of employment in the slate quarry in the years immediately before 1871 was partly responsible.

Other factors which affected island fishing were the coming of the railway to Reenard, on the mainland opposite the island, and the demand for fish for the American and British markets. The American market was very important from 1890 onwards, making it worthwhile for the local merchant, Alexander O'Driscoll, to travel to New York in 1906 to find out why a lot of fish from the island could not be sold there. He concluded that the consignment had suffered from careless handling before it left Ireland; this may have led him to consider setting up a proper factory and looking for a grant from the Department of Agriculture towards the cost. His request was refused, possibly because of objections from one of his neighbours.

At this period, Valentia had 45 seine boats and 158 men employed, who caught in 1891 375,590 mackerel, 198,000 herrings, over 3 ton of cod, ling and hake and more than 2 ton of other fish. Nearly all the fresh mackerel and herring went to the English markets as well as some of the scad, ling and hake. 118 barrels of mackerel were cured, each weighing 200 lbs net weight, and containing 240 mackerel, mostly for the American market, where they fetched £3 to £4 per barrel. The catches varied considerably from year to year, because the previous year, in 1890, double the number of mackerel were caught but only one quarter the number of herrings. The erection of a pier at Tinnies by the Board of Trinity College around this time was of considerable help to its tenants there.

The Congested Districts Board did much to encourage and improve fishing. The Board paid £2,000 to erect a pier at Tragannane, on the road down to the lighthouse. It was designed by James Hack Tuke, a Quaker engineer, who was involved in local government for a long period. Its location was very controversial to judge from the comments of those who later gave evidence to the Board, but it was much used. Alex O'Driscoll, the local merchant already mentioned, thought it "perfectly useless" but then he was very critical of all the Board's efforts. He wanted the Board to finance the purchase of a "steam drifter" but they supplied "Zulus, yawls and even curraghs", all of which he claimed had been discarded by other people. Another witness, William J. Delap, wasn't so sure about the steam- drifter, mainly because it would necessitate new piers. The only point on which everyone who gave evidence to the Board agreed was that there was no local capital to buy a steam-drifter and that the Board should give loans to help.

The islanders must have been regarded by the Board as skilled fisherman because in the early years of its work, Rev. William Spotswood Green, the fishery expert, brought boats, nets and men from Valentia district to Clifden and Cleggan in Co. Galway to teach the people the system of mackerel fishing by means of seine nets, with best results. The Board was also willing to contribute £7,000 towards the cost of a new pier at Knightstown, but in fact this money was never expended, possibly because of World War I.

Seine boats and "followers" at the quay, Knightstown about 1900.

After 1900 the number of mackerel around the Irish coast seems to have increased and gradually the quality of boats improved. In 1912 the first paraffin Kelvin-engine boat built in the south of Ireland was brought to the island by T. Galvin, who also owned the hotel in Knightstown. However, mackerel prices were low and in that year fetched only 14/- per 120. As many as 500,000 mackerel were a common daily landing for all the Valentia boats together. In the month of September 1927, 7,000 barrels of mackerel were shipped from Valentia Harbour, but from this onwards the catches diminished or, as the islanders put it, "the fish went away".

At this time also, the American Government imposed a tariff on all imported fish which greatly upset the Irish export market. In the 1940s T.W. O'Connell was the last man to export a consignment of mackerel.

Fishing was a hard life and a dangerous one. In the days of open boats, whether rowed or with sails like "Yawls", men had to be tough to row for long periods and in all weathers. Not much remains in island folklore about the yawls but, to quote Dermot Ring, who helped in supplying much of the information in this chapter, "stories about seine boats would fill a separate book". They were open carvel-built wooden boats approximately 33ft long and 6'6 wide at beam. They varied a little but not enough to exclude them from regatta regulations and it was most important to be able to compete and win in the annual regattas. The size of the boat created a problem between the boatbuilders and the families who owned them. The shipwright was anxious that the boats would be safe, sea-worthy and "sea-kindly", while the owners were just as anxious that the boats be fast, so that they could show off their prowess as oarsmen to the best advantage. The seine-boat had to carry a crew of 13 or 14, 6 or 7 heavy oars, and the net itself, which weighed a ton when wet. The boats were "fine" enough if they measured at 33' by 6'6; the design could be changed to make them more speedy to satisfy the whim of a proud family, but this could prove to be dangerous. The second boat, or "follower" was smaller and carried six oarsmen on single oars and the cox. The seine-boat had clamp-oars, square where they rested in the dowels, with two men on each oar. These oars were not feathered when rowing. The "follower" had rounded oars. The instructions from the helmsman were always in Irish, even after English became the everyday language of the fishermen.

The main seine fishing seasons were Spring and August to October, which were also the times of sowing and harvesting and, most important of all, the period when extra income came into the households. It also meant that if the men were at sea most of the farm work had to be done by the women. It isn't possible to estimate how many fishermen were farmers as well but all but the poorest held some land.

Peter FitzGerald, later to become the 19th Knight of Kerry, gave evidence to the Commission on Poverty in 1837, that fishermen were considered by some landlords as unsuitable tenants, because they devoted too much time to fishing instead of looking after their land. Fishermen often had to pay higher rents because their land, being nearer the shore, required less back-breaking labour in carrying sand and sea-weed from the shore to manure their potato patches.

Sometimes 4-oar boats fished without the seine-boat. They could be used when the weather was too rough and later in the season when the big shoals had broken up or gone far out to sea. The smaller boat was also the one on which the men sometimes made a fire to cook their potatoes or fish. The larger seine-boat was too crowded with men and nets to make a fire in a pot with safety. A favourite meal was scad, or horse-mackerel, and they kept the offal for fertiliser. Horse mackerel could also provide oil for lighting. It may have smelled when lit, but it was free in an economy where candles and paraffin oil had to be paid for.

At the end of the nineteenth century, up to 40 four-oar boats fished for mackerel out of Tragannane, and Dohilla, going north along the coast. The area between Reenadrolaun (the Wren's Point) and the lighthouse was famous for this type of fishing and provided a livelihood for numerous families. In 1900 there were 100 smacks fishing in Valentia but some of these were foreign. The extract from the Census of 1901 shows that on the night of 31st March there were 13 Manx vessels in Valentia Harbour as well as two from Arklow and one from Newry, Co. Down.

The same Census gives a clear picture of the ages of the fishermen and what part of the island they came from. Tinnies Lower West had only one family who fished, out of a total of 16 occupied houses. Coarhabeg had three families; James Casey was 62 and fished with his son, also James, who was only 21; the others were Patrick Donoghue who was 28 and married and Thomas Foley, also 28, who was single. Sons did not necessarily follow their father's occupation. The father of Thomas Foley from Coarhabeg was an agricultural labourer. In Dohilla, under the Slate Quarry, Michael Donaghue was a fisherman but his father, Peter, was a mason. John Neill, who also fished, was the son of a farmer and quarryman. In Knightstown village, only James Shea, who was 70, described himself as a fisherman but there were a number of boatmen and ferrymen as well as a boat-builder, Con Murphy. Some of the older fishermen in 1901 could neither read nor write but this was fairly common in all the population over 60. All the fishermen could speak both Irish and English.

The names of some of the great seine-boats and their crews have survived. "The Lady Butler", "The Brothers Hope", "the Blue Bird", and "The Up Kerry" are quoted and crews like that of Johnny Mahony will never be seen again. Men talked of Round Oars and Clamp Oars, of "scol-raws" and "Doul-pins" and "Doorneens" and they were admired for their skills as fishermen and as oarsmen.

Prices were high for fish at the turn of the century. £1 to £1.10.0 per 120 mackerel was common but it even reached as high as £2.12.0 per 120. The fish were sold in "casts", three casts of 40 making up the 120, but the prices paid were actually for 126 fish because six were always "thrown in" for the buyer. The newspaper, *The Kerry Sentinel*, reported on 25th April 1900:

> Valentia is alive with the business connected with the fishing industry and very good wages are paid to all employed in boxing and removing the fish to the railway station for conveyance to the English markets. Some is also sent by steamer to England. Two Norwegian barges have come with cargoes of ice. Valentia has established itself as a great fishing station.

A Lawrence photograph shows the hulk in the harbour on which the ice was stored. These old ships were later used for storing coal.

Descriptions of the harbour at its busiest vary. Local tradition says that there were so many boats that it was possible to walk across to Beginnish, one of two small islands located in Valentia Harbour, travelling from one boat to the next. A Blasket Islander, who visited Valentia about 1890 to collect a curragh, described "the greatest sight of masts any of us had ever seen. All these masts were on big ships or little vessels, for fishing boats had collected there from far and near that year after mackerel. Plenty of money was being made and the poor themselves didn't want for a pound".

Today seine boats are used for racing on Regatta Day and it is doubtful if any one would survive one night's rowing, or attempt to row a four-oar boat to the Skelligs.

Because there are now only a few survivors of seine boat crews, it is important to record the actual sequence of the fishing. Two positions were most important, the captain and the "Spier", or "look-out", and such men were highly regarded in the community. The seine net had heavy rings and a rope called the "brail" going through the rings. It was leaded at the bottom so that it would sink and was corked at the top where it would float. The boats also had to carry counter-balance weights, usually old 56 lb iron weights, and a quantity of small flat beachstones about 4" by 1". There was also a wooden block about 2 ft long and about 9" square. A 12" lip was cut out about half way and an iron bolt with a wheel that rolled inserted to take the "brail" rope. The weights were placed in the centre of the boat along the keel line and the stones were placed in the bows of the seine boat.

The Harbour at Knightstown with Hulks for storing ice in the background. c. 1900

When the "Spier", or look-out, shouted "Barriasc", he had seen the light created in the water by the fish shoaling, making the phosphorescent glow on the surface of the sea. The area of the light indicated the amount of the fish and this could be acres in area. The colour of the shoal indicated whether or not it was mackerel.

The first order from the Captain of the seine-boat was to the follower to take the rope of the net, making the "hold on". The seine oarsmen then gave all the speed in their power away from the follower. The two men on the aft or stroke oar did not row as they were fully occupied. They had to shoot the seine net over the side of the boat while it was going at full speed, around as much fish as they could circumvent, completing a full circle between the two boats. The most skilled stage of the operation was to complete the last part of the circle without allowing the fish to escape before the ends of the seine could be brought together. At this point, the Spier in the bows of the seine boat tossed the small stones into the area not yet sealed, frightening the fish back into the net. As well as using the stones, some of the oarsmen on the inside of the circle "poled" their oars. This meant shooting the heavy oars, blade first, straight down towards the sea floor. The oar would then shoot back in the same place. The second man had an iron block tied to a rope that he threw out and pulled up and down, also controlling the fish.

When the two boats met, the "bunt" rope at the top of the net was pulled tight thus making a bag or purse of the net, with the fish inside. At this stage , the "follower" went round to the opposite side of the seine net. The crew grabbed hold of the net up against the side of the boat. In the seine boat the men were busy hanging out the weights as counterbalances on the far side of the boat, otherwise the heavy net would have overturned the boat. The full seine "purse" was then hauled over the side of the boat, first filling the follower and the extra into the seine. If there were some fish still left in the net the captain might give the spare fish to other boats or he could decide to tow the net with the remaining fish in it back to base. This was another tricky operation, depending on the distance, the tides and the calmness of the sea and, of course, the condition of his nets. Old or much repaired nets would not bear the strain of a long tow.

The seine was said to be 120 yards long and nearly 30 yards deep. Small mesh cotton net was used. The "bunt" rope was hemp and ran the full length of the boat, easing out at the edges, called the "sleeves". There were rings all along the rope and another rope went through the rings to make the purse of the seine.

When the boats got to the point of sale, they either bargained with the buyer or, more usually, they supplied the same buyer each day, having an agreement with him for an average price. The buyer supplied the fish boxes to the pier and the crew counted the fish into the boxes, another tedious job at the end of a long night's work.

The fishermen always brought home some fish for family and neighbours. They were very generous men and rarely passed a poor neighbour or a widow without giving them some fish, often a "strap" as they called 12 or 14 fish hung on a cord or piece of line passed under the gills of the fish and through the mouth.

There is no one alive today to tell whether the same kind of net was always used but one nineteenth century account stated that Valentia fishermen used a finer net than other south-coast areas. Sir Peter FitzGerald's voluminous correspondence includes an order dated 21st July 1878 for 80 yards of 280 meshes of the 50 row 18 ply cotton net same as sample, and it was to be barked; 40 yards 20 score 54 row 2 ply of barked cotton netting and 20 yards 15 score 45 row 21 ply, all to be forwarded as soon as possible. It would seem from this order that various nets were used and perhaps none of the above meshes were for seine fishing. Glanleam House had its own seine boat but the quantity ordered would appear to be for more then one boat. Perhaps the nets were sold by the Knight to his tenants. Nets were also stated to be purchased in Cahirciveen and nets were made by the fishermen themselves.

The "barking" of the nets with oakum was a big undertaking and was the occasion for a "meitheal", a group of family and neighbours, who came together to help with the tasks which would have been outside the capacity of an ordinary family. One of the venues for the barking was on the strand at Glanleam. In the far corner today is a huge iron pot set in concrete with space underneath for a fire. This is where the nets were boiled in water with the oakum melted in it. A number of strong men would have been needed for the operation.

The fishermen were good judges of the weather and knew when to watch for the "Madra Gaoithe", the cloud formation which preceded a series of violent storms, but they were not always able to foretell danger and there were a number of drownings. Eight young men from the island lost their lives in a storm in Dingle Bay in 1908, and the following year there was an even greater tragedy. Liam Mc Gabhann, who was born and reared on the island, became a famous journalist, and he has left a moving account of the tragedy.:

The women in their shawls helped the men get the long seine nets aboard and they bent their backs too, as the boat with its six clamped oars rowed by twelve men, for speed purposes, hit the water's edge.

They then lowered the "Leanai", or as the English called her, the "follower", though it was forbidden by tradition to speak in anything but Gaelic while fishing.

The leanai had six oars also, but only one man on each oar. It was the seine-boat which would make speed as they chased the barr-iasc, the phosphorescent toplights of the mackerel shoals that would shine under the dark-moon (the dubh-re).

The women carefully placed the holy-water bottles under the bowsheeting before the boats floated and they walked slowly up the strand as the oars flashed and the boats joined the black fleets heading out for the harbour outlet at the lighthouse.

The Portmagee boat, with John Devane and his crew, was the last of the line, because he and his eighteen men had to travel further. And there being no moon, nobody in any boat remarked that there was a darkening over the western mountain. They could not tell, then, that a mad wind was rushing up from Biscay.

It was heavy dusk when John Devane and his crew, including his son and his cousins, shot their trawl just where the tides meet off Thrawnaboolla. The mackerel lights they had just seen making a strange glow in the harbour came from thousands of fish which had rushed before the agitation in Biscay. But they were not to know that. They were alone. The equinoctal gale struck. John Devane stood petrified in the helm.

The thousands of gleaming things that had risen in his dark nets between the seine-boat and the leanai had suddenly become a myriad menace. The long years of saving for these boats and these nets flashed suddenly through his mind and were dashed out of his ken by the shock of the wind and the waves.

"Fan sa talamh" (steer towards the land) he had shouted, urging his men to pull for the doubtful shelter of the Bouille Point. But the nets and their load of taunting silver held them back.

81

"Saidh an bord teas, go leir" (all pull on the port oars) he shouted, but they didn't hear him. They could not pull on the port oars because the long poles (the oars) were caught in the laden nets.

A flash of lightening lit up John Devane's frightened face as he gave the last order "Gearraidh na lionthai" -- Cut the nets! But the follower's crew were already in the sea, gasping and groping, trammelled in the strangling web. Ironically, it was the weight of the fish more than the shock of the storm that had heeled the follower over.

John Devane felt the waters sucking at his body and he swam in terror to his son.

Into the horror of it came other voices. It was the will of God the neighbours said that Mike Cahill's boats came on the Portmagee men.

But from the maelstrom of the sea they could only save eleven. Eleven men exhausted into unconsciousness. It was almost dawn when Cahill's rowed wearily into the harbour. They laid the survivors out on the pier and the doctor began the work of recovering them. Women who heard the shouting from the shore, above the storm, shrieked and wailed."

Fishermen were great drinkers and perhaps they needed to be to survive the long nights rowing and maybe come in to snatch a few hours sleep, and if the harvest was in danger, get up to help cut hay or save turf. If there was time, a visit to Knightstown's bar or the Royal Hotel was a must. A new barmaid at the Hotel was sceptical when one man came in and ordered 21 pints. She refused to draw them until the owner, Timothy Galvin, came on the scene and told her it was alright. It was common to send one man up ahead of the rest of the crew to order for them while they were occupied securing the nets on the quay. There was method in this, because it took a long time to draw that much porter properly.

Another oft-quoted fact about the fishermen was that they were all highly superstitious. To see a red-haired woman on the way to the boats was considered the height of bad luck. Older women today remember as children being hunted in to the house when a group of fishermen were seen coming down the road.

At the height of the fishing, just before World War I, every boy leaving school could expect to make a living from fishing provided he was strong enough for the work. He simply looked about for a place in a suitable boat. Sometimes a young man might be called in to fill a gap in a crew, but usually in a follower, which was not such heavy work. A Mahony, one of the family of famous fishermen at Ardcost on the mainland, recalled that he was only 14 or so when he went to sea for the first time. Word came to Ardcost that there were shoals of mackerel seen east of Ceannglass outside Cuanunna Harbour. They were so short-handed, they put the young lads into the follower, with Mahony being one of them. Come the dawn, they had no fish and the captain ordered a rope to be put aboard the follower, to tow her home and so take to weight off the young lads. Rounding Ceannglass, another seine boat came up outside them and challenged them for fishing in their waters. The Ardcost seine cast off the follower and went away, hell for leather. The wind freshened from the south-west, and it took the young lads in the follower half the day to round Dolus Head and make Ardcost, sick and wet to the skin. To quote the young man "There was no sense in it, we were too young for that game".

Apart from the money made by the fishermen, there was a thriving industry in fishing. The women who cleaned, gutted and packed earned wages, as did the cooper, the fish-box maker, the basket makers, and the men who loaded the barrels on to the steamers. After the coming of the railway to Reenard, there was work for the carters who brought the fish from the boats to the train.

A photograph from the Lawrence collection, though it was taken at Portmagee, on the mainland, shows the entire process. The young girls in shawls, on the right-hand side, are all "splitters". The girls stood on opposite sides of the table, on one side the splitter and on the other the "gutter". Behind was a vat for washing, very important because if all the blood was not washed off, the salted fish would rot. The fish were taken out of the vat and placed into boxes to dry and then transferred to the tables to be salted and packed. Splitters were a little better paid than the other workers, but gutters had the hardest job. Because these girls had to dip their hands into the salt, the skin became raw and had to be bandaged. After two weeks the mackerel were repacked into final barrels and then the brine had to be topped up, about twice a week, until the steamer came. This was done with a special can which had a long pipe and which can be seen in the hand of the boy in a cap in the Lawrence photograph. The barrels were loaded on the steamer, two at a time. The women were paid about 10/- per week at the beginning of this century. Baskets were made then by Mike Shea and Tom Murphy who grew the sally rods for making them as well. The island women were regarded as being relatively prosperous; as contemporary photographs show, they could afford shoes.

Fish curing at Portmagee.

The workers' conditions were better than at Portmagee or Coonunna because the disused Slate Yard in Knightstown had plenty of roofed buildings and it was never necessary for workers there to operate in the open. Johnny Driscoll was the island cooper in the 1920s and if extra help was needed he would get a Galivan from Ballinskelligs to help.

John Shea, who is now in his eighties, recalls that "it was back-breaking work. When 40,000 to 50,000 fish came in one day, the women and the men worked all day, that night, and part of the next day until all the fish were gutted and in the water. The workers were paid by the day and would get a little extra plus food if they worked overtime."

The men who fished in the seine boats wore heavy oil-skins. At one period these came from Yarmouth and were so tough you couldn't get a knife through them. When that supply dried up early this century, a local woman, John Cahill's wife, made them; this was even better, because men could then get a suit "made to measure". The calico was bought in Cahirciveen, brought home on fair day, boiled in linseed oil and other ingredients like glycerine, until it was completely waterproof. The men tied the trousers tight at the ankles and were even known to carry their fish home tucked in the ends of their trousers.

Apart from the fish exported, much was consumed at home and every house had two barrels of salted fish, which provided a welcome addition to the food supply and added relish to the staple diet of potatoes and milk or buttermilk. Fish were also put up the chimney to be smoked and the "yellow mackerel", as it was then called, made a beautiful meal. Hake was very plentiful during World War I, so that the men then fished for them with lines while waiting for their nets to fill. The salted fish was used during the winter, but when fresh fish was available, it was preferred. One housewife let the neighbours know that she could offer a choice when she shouted to her husband "Will you have fresh or salted for your dinner today?"

Barrels on the quay at Knightstown waiting for loading on the steamer. c. 1890

The fastest oarsmen were from Beginnish, the small island between Valentia and the mainland at Dolus Head to the north. They had established a shelter, "The Pilot's Lookout", on the western extremity of the island so that they could be the first to spot the mainsails of approaching vessels and therefore would be the first to meet the incoming ship; the first out was awarded the job of piloting the ship into harbour and of course this service had to be paid for. The McCrohan family became the acknowledged official pilots at one time.

Chapter Eight
Life in the Big House.

Glanleam was a "Big House" rather than a "Great House", and like all landlord's houses it was run by a considerable staff. Drawings of servants "Peggy Donoghue" "Kate" and "Judy" are taken from the FitzGerald papers about 1850. Peggy Donoghue "the flower of Glanleam" was described as "for many years the kitchen maid and was for many years a family pensioner". The doggerel about her said:

> She stews down my heart and she fries up my liver,
> And in many soft breasts my Peg sticks a skewer,
> Many women to keep one lover are toiling,
> My Peg sets the whole tribe of Murphy's a-boiling,
> In chamber, in Parlour, in kitchen, in hall,
> She glows with exertion to benefit all,
> When we're cold she brings warmth,
> she brings light when it's dark,
> And is wise as an owl, tho' she's up with the lark.
> The fires on our hearth respond to her skill,
> And our beds would be comfortless only for her.

Jane is described as "our superior dairy-maid sent from Ballywalter". She is pictured with her "dash churn", in which butter was made by dashing a paddle up and down in the churn, a tiring and time-consuming task.

Kate Latch is described as "a wild Celt" , and there was "a bit of romance between her and a Sullivan of Gortgower".

Mr. Pickwick was probably the butler, or the valet. Dan O'Sullivan (Bat) seems to have been the local poacher, rather than one of the Glanleam servants. His name "Cassure" shows that he belonged to the O'Sullivan clan nicknamed "Hammer", which distinguished that branch of the family from the "brogs" (shoes) and the "Coom Baghs", this being their battle cry.

The kitchen-maid and the milk-maid, about 1840.

The FitzGerald daughters were educated by various governesses, some of whose names survive; Miss Guise was probably French or Swiss, and there is also mention of Adele Whitehouse who wrote to the children in 1858 that she did not like her new "place" half as much as Valentia.

The boys had tutors and some went to Harrow as did various cousins including the Talbot Crosbies. A letter from Maurice FitzGerald to his mother in November 1855 apologised for a bad school report; he asked permission for a Talbot-Crosbie cousin to come to stay at Glanleam after Christmas and he thanked for pots of jam. He sent his regards to "all at home including Miss Hickson" (the governess). Later letters from Harrow were in simple French and Maurice informed his family that he was "becoming proficient in German".

The children used "pet names" when writing to their parents and Peter in turn wrote to "Dolly Dowse and Em" describing the journey from

Dublin to Holyhead and the railway to Bangor, where the new bridge was being built.

Peter FitzGerald's children left accounts of "feeding sparrows from the FitzGerald's window" and of "drawing trees". They were great collectors of ferns, usually with the Blackburns, the children of the Slate Quarry manager, with whom they were very friendly.

The Blackburns lived first in the house at Coombe Road, now the O'Driscoll's, and later in the house in Knightstown, where the sub-office of the Allied Irish Bank is today. They would have been near enough to Glanleam for regular visiting. Fanny FitzGerald found a fern called "moonwort" and the next day the Blackburns found one called "adder's tongue". Mary FitzGerald wrote to "dearest papa" in 1850 that Helen Blackburn gave her the leaves of a fern which she had not had before and claimed that they had got "all the different kinds that grow on the island". They also grew strawberries.

The children often wrote to Papa when he was away and sent presents like the violet grown in their own garden. Storms were described and wreckage and "a dog-fish found on the strand" was to be put in whiskey. A flower garden was being made for Fanny. When one sees the profusion of flowers growing wild on the island today, the interest in botany is not surprising and of course, it was one of the "ladylike" occupations approved for Victorian women. One islander became an international figure in the world of plants. Susan Lecky, whose father was the manager of the Quarry after Blackburn, made three drawings of *Pinguicula Vulgaris* and *P. Grandiflora*, found in Co. Cork and Co. Kerry, and *P.Lusitanica* from Valentia Island. These were presented to the Royal Botanic Gardens at Kew in 1917 and were later exhibited there in the North Gallery. Susan Lecky died in London in 1896.

The gardens at Glanleam were famous; according to Nangle's *Guide to Trees and Shrubs for Ireland* published in 1908 "embothrium, coccineum or Chilean Fire Bush", with its profusion of scarlet fire-like flowers in May-June, was normally a shrub but there was a great specimen of some 60 feet on Valentia.

The FitzGerald children were also encouraged to be charitable. They were making "alumettes" to sell to try to make enough money to "get a shirt for the little boy that leads his blind mother".

Hallowe'en was a very important celebration. Various references to dunking for apples appear in the family papers and celebrations with the Blackburns were followed by snap-apples for the staff.

The present structure at Glanleam is only a portion of the nineteenth century house. About a third was demolished in the early 1930s, but an original picture shows the house in its entirety, with the highly cultivated walled garden very visible. Accounts of the numbers of the outdoor staff vary but the figure of 30 men working on the estate farm and gardens is often quoted. Peaches, nectarines and even grapes were grown in the hot-houses for family consumption and in the later period produce from Glanleam was sent to the other FitzGerald houses in England. Gifts of fruit and game also went to other landlords. At the turn of the century, special gifts were sent to a sanatorium in England.

Glanleam in its hey-day.

The game-keeper on Irish estates was always an outsider; presumably any locals would have too many poacher relatives. Thomas Tapper, the game-keeper at Glanleam, was English and is very kindly remembered by Nora O'Sullivan. Because her father was a good shot he would accompany Tapper; as a result the Sunday dinner in O'Sullivan's in the season was often curlew, plover, duck or redshank. The *soighini* (delicacies) grouse, snipe, and woodcock would have been kept for the Knight's table.

Glanleam was not a typical landlord's house because a large amount of its fitments came from the slate in the local quarry. The contents at the time of the auction in 1925 included fenders, fireplaces and tables of local slate and the garden had seats and tables. The steps in front of the hall-door were also slate. Reenglass, the FitzGerald Dower House, had similar furnishings, including very attractive slate shelves.

The family bedrooms were all called after flowers: escalonia, Choisya, daffodil, myrtle, Helitrope, Verbena, azalea, fuchsia, Veronica, as well as ivy and Arbutus. There were seven other bedrooms and a cubicle, kitchen and scullery, servants' hall, laundry, washhouse, dairy, butter pantry, a Butler's room, cellar, larder, yard and bike house and various outhouses including a golf pavilion. The reception rooms included a morning room, a study, a lobby, a drawing room, a dining room and a studio. The tennis and croquet equipment and the boats sold at the auction give some idea of how much sporting activity went on.

In the first half of the nineteenth century Maria, the first wife of Maurice, the 18th Knight, tried to give employment to the local women. The flax growing introduced in the previous years meant that there were supplies available for linen weaving. This was encouraged and also a mixture of wool and linen. Not much information survives of where the fabrics were sold or how much money was generated; probably only enough clothes were made for home consumption. Certainly flax was spun and woven on the island, there being a different type of spinning wheel for flax and for wool.

Later industries are very well documented. Reenglass, the large house on the coast road, is reputed to have been built as a dower house for the widow of the Knight and was later lived in by the unmarried FitzGerald daughters. A two-storey stone house in the grounds was used as a "Knitting House" and from about 1880 onwards was the centre of a thriving, well-managed industry.

During the minor famine of 1880, a relief committee was formed on the island which suggested that a sum of money be voted to promote knitting amongst the older women and young girls. Miss Frances FitzGerald undertook the administration of the grant, and, procuring good patterns, started the work. The knitters improved rapidly and earnings varied according to the season and spare time from farm work. Eight years after the industry had been set up, there were eighty workers on the books, all from the island.

In 1888 the catalogue of goods at the Exhibition organised by Lady Aberdeen, the wife of the Viceroy, at 57 Dawson St, Dublin had only one entry for the entire County Kerry. Miss FitzGerald, of Valentia Island, offered Jerseys at 4s/6d and 12/6 each, Stockings 1/8 to 4/6 per pair. Socks were 1/- to 1/9 per pair, and gloves 1/6 to 2/6 per pair.

The same year, an advertisement in Helen Blackburn's book, *A Handybook of Reference for Irishwomen* published for the Irish Exhibition at Olympia in London, offered much the same knitted goods to be purchased from Miss Frances FitzGerald of Glanleam, but there was an additional item of shooting stockings at 4/6 a pair.

For the Ui Breasil Exhibition in Dublin in 1911, The Valentia Island Industries Stall decided to join with Caherdaniel Branch. Miss FitzGerald was president and was then residing at Reenglass and she intended to exhibit handknitted jerseys and socks. Mrs Alice Higgins of Cool sent home-spun tweeds, Mrs Daniel O'Sullivan an Irish Cloak, Miss Hannah Dennehy, handknitted knicker hose. Other island exhibitors were Miss Brigid Dennehy, Mrs C. O'Shea and Mrs Alice O'Connor.

The wool was purchased by Miss FitzGerald in bulk and her accounts show that 12 lbs cost 20/6 to 31/6 and included Paton's, worsted yarn, jersey yarn, fingering, shamrock fingering, merino white, and alloa whelking. Unfortunately, we do not know where the supplies of wool were purchased.

The payments for knitting shown below were included in Emily FitzGerald's papers but Frances seems to have been the most involved. It was to Miss F. FitzGerald that the invitation was sent by the Plunkett Presentation Committee to be present at Plunkett House in Merrion Square, Dublin, on the occasion of the formal presentation to the Right Hon. Sir Horace Plunkett on 11th November 1908. Sir Horace was the founder of the Co-Operative Movement.

Details of the size of a jersey in Emily FitzGerald's papers give the measurements in centimetres so some of the knitting may have sold on the continent. The family had contacts everywhere and at the end of the last century and in the early years of this century the women were receiving invitations to weddings in London, and Menton Alpes. In 1894

Emily had been in France to take a "Cours de Musique Vocale" so may have sold some of the island products there. Island tradition is that socks were knit for the White Star Liners and for the Mental Hospital in Killarney. A list of goods consigned to the Hudson Bay Company about this period included "Valentia vests".

The postal service from Valentia must have been better in 1888 than it is today. Miss FitzGerald, Miss Delap, the daughter of the Church of Ireland clergyman, and Mrs Sullivan of Ballyhearny all advertised in Helen Blackburn's book what they could supply through the post. Butter, cream cheese, eggs, fish, scallops, lobsters, honey, kippered pollock, and flowers such as daffodils, violets, and arum lillies were all offered at prices like 1/- to 1/2 per lb. for butter and 3d each for the kippered pollock. Presumably, the unmarried daughters of the landlord and the rector were glad to find ways of supplementing their incomes. They are all remembered for their charitable work for the hospital, and the provision of food and entertainment at the Fisherman's Hall. Miss Delap is recorded as visiting the Island and Coast Society School but all these activities would have produced no income.

The wives of the Knights left no written accounts themselves but certain details of their lives appear in the children's correspondence to their father. They went on holidays to England. Mama went to Torquay in December 1858 and there are letters to Miss FitzGerald at the Bilton Hotel, in Sackville Street, Dublin. There are pages of family photographs taken in the south of France and Switzerland. Travelling so far did not seem to be a problem and the distance was not so serious when they stayed for months on end rather than weeks.

Life was made more interesting by the constant stream of visitors and of course there were always the relations to visit. An invitation to dine in Dingle preserved in the National Library Papers in Dublin shows how far away the Knight was expected to travel but presumably he stayed over night. The distance by boat in one of the large yachts would not have been a problem. Spring Rice cousins were doubly or trebly related to the FitzGeralds and seem to have spent time at Glanleam before they owned property in the village. Two FitzGerald children and two Spring Rices all died within a month of one another in 1875, a year when there was an epidemic of some sort. It is remembered that the parish priest died that year too.

Some idea of the style and elegance at Glanleam around the beginning of this century can be got from the staff employed there in 1901. The indoor staff numbered 14! The housekeeper was Mary Boulding from Co. Armagh, and she was Church of Ireland. The lady's maid was a French widow, aged 29 and a Roman Catholic. The "Nurse Domestic" was 55 and from Shropshire; Rose Freeman, the Cook Domestic, was from Derbyshire; Eilly Phelby, the kitchen maid was from Buckinghamshire; the housemaids were local, Annie and Bessie O'Donoghue, both Catholic; Nellie Burke, the Dairymaid-domestic was from Cork and so was Aileen Daly; Nora Dineen, the 18-year-old scullery maid was from Kerry but the butler, William Cooper, was from Warwickshire. John Clark, the 19-year-old valet, hailed from London; Frederick Gillen, the footman, came from Bath and John Jones, the groom, from Welshpool. These last may have been part of the staff of the other FitzGerald houses, brought to Ireland to supplement the regular staff.

Even when the family moved their permanent home to Berkshire in England, the house at Glanleam was kept for holidays.

It is still remembered on the island that there was an excellent dairy at Glanleam; that the cows all had stalls with syphonic feeding system and that their lactation records were over each stall; that Glanleam animals won prizes at the Royal Dublin Society Shows and that the farm was "like a little Agricultural college".

Chapter Nine
Women's Lives

Because farming wives were the largest group in the island population they merit taking separately. To quote Mrs O'Donoghue in Feaghmaan "the women were the backbone of the farming economy and where they were no good, the families went under."

The daily routine of the women's lives on small farms probably did not change much from the last century until the coming of machinery, the advent of the creamery in 1939, rural electrification, the replacement by the range of the open fire and of course, running water.

Another change was the availability of relatively cheap mass-produced clothes, very different from earlier times when every garment, even handkerchiefs, had to be made at home. Parcels of clothes from America were also a help.

After the middle of the nineteenth century, women no longer walked the roads of Munster "spalpeening", the custom for men and women from the poor mountainous areas to go to save the harvest in the rich lowlands of North Kerry and Counties Limerick, Cork and Tipperary. They left their homes on Valentia before day-break to get the ferry and walk to Killarney the first day -- their boots held by their whangs (leather laces) slung across their shoulders -- barefoot, saving the boots for the stubble fields and for Sunday.

The earliest account of women's work on the island comes from Arseneth Nicholson, an American, who visited Valentia in March 1845. She arrived in Ireland to distribute bible tracts but did not mention distributing them on the island. She

.. walked this morning to the coast opposite Valentia. Here both men and women go out in boats to gather from the rocks seaweed which is used for manure. They take a long pole with hooks upon the end, and wade in, and scrape the weed from the rocks; put it in boats and the men take it ashore. At night they take a basketful upon their backs and bend toward their wretched cabins to boil the potatoes and lie down upon the straw; and in the morning wake to the same hopes and so to the same employment. Woman is here worse off then the beast of burden, because she is often made to do what a beast never does.

Tradition on the island supports the Nicholson description. Each family had a defined "strand" on the foreshore for seaweed. They brought the weed to the water's edge and then brought it home when it suited, in packs on women's backs, being kept in place by a band across the forehead. Seaweed was even brought up the face of the cliff at Foilhomurrum, a feat which today would be regarded as a test for climbing Mount Everest.

Men were known to vet possible wives for the strength of their backs and one story tells of a man being interviewed by the parish priest when he proposed to marry a girl considerably younger then himself. The P.P. suggested that the match was unsuitable but the man replied: "Sure Father, if I don't get a wife this year I'll have to buy a donkey." As well as seaweed women were known to carry creels of turf on their backs and at one time the families living in Dohilla, under the Slate Quarry, carried turf on a pathway across the face of the cliff under Geokaun by what was known as the "iron gate" because it saved the long walk round by the road from the turf-banks at Culloo.

Before the Great Famine, in the 1830s, cottages are described as being "13 ft long by 10 broad, the walls 6ft high and built of stone and mud; they contained generally only one apartment and the roof was merely thatch composed of straw or potato stalks but in most cases kept out the rain. The floor was made of beaten earth and was commonly damp, being below the level of the surrounding ground and below the water contained in manure holes outside the doors. There were no chimneys in general though some had a "sort of basket above a hole in the roof." A few of the newest built at that time had a chimney flue up the wall made of sticks and mud.

The windows had no glass and many of the very worst had no proper door, only a "kind of hurdle with heather or long grass woven among sticks".

A very graphic description of conditions for women was given in the years just after the Great Famine. Harriet Martineau, English of Quaker stock, was appalled by the cabins in the groups often called "Clahanes" which existed at Clynacartan, and Craugh and where the granite cross overlooking Glanleam is today. There were at least three such villages all long since disappeared. These were the one-roomed houses of landless men who worked as labourers when they could get work. According to Harriet Martineau:

> The thatched roofs are rounded and have no eaves; the dwellings are usually set down one before another; so that a hamlet has the appearance from a little distance, that we noticed in the little fishing villages of Achill, of a cluster of Hottentot kraals. In our eyes, they were less respectable than Indian wigwams, because of their darkness, and the infamous filth surrounding them, in the hollows in which they are sunk.

Harriet Martineau saw "the housewife sitting down to milk her cow (by her own fireside literally) and the donkey putting his head out of the cottage door, going forth for his morning meal; he has waited until the dew is off the grass. The children, still hot and heavy with sleep, in their rags, the same they have slept in, are a disgusting sight to the traveller".

The account of the cabins left by the FitzGerald children shows that Harriet Martineau was not exaggerating.

Not all the houses were as bad as the cabins. O'Donoghue's house in Feaghmaan is 200-years-old and was always a substantial two storey "cross" house, meaning that it was more than a rectangle. Until the 1930s the upstairs had windows at the ends only. The present dormer windows gave extra space.

Apart from the Knight's residence at Glanleam, there were in 1837 substantial houses at Coarhabeg, occupied by Capt. Spotswood, and at Ballymanagh which was the occasional residence of Miles Mahony of Cullina. Other large houses were Reenellen in Knightstown, originally occupied by the family of the Church of Ireland rector, Reenglass, the Dower House of the FitzGeralds, the Revenue House, the Rectory in

Knightstown, and the two substantial houses on the front facing the Harbour, in one of which Blackburns and later Leckys lived. The number of ruined substantial farmhouses still visible is surprising and proves that there were cabins and substantial farmhouses all over the island.

A favourite walk for the Cable Staff. Mollie O'Sullivan and her daughter at Primrose Dell in Reenglass - the knitting house can be seen in the background.

Most farms on the island were small, the grass of "2 to 4 cows, or 6 to 8 cows" being often the people's measurement.

Women's work included the raising of bonhams, hens and turkeys for sale which was an important part of the family economy. Geese were reared because they ate everything, including raw potatoes, but they needed to be watched because they had a high consumption of water. Once the Creamery came to the island, the geese were discontinued. They destroyed the grass which was needed for the cattle and were therefore uneconomic. Turkeys were another cash crop for the farming wives. One woman was able to buy a cart and harness out of her turkey money and a cart was a luxury for smaller farmers.

At the beginning of this century small farmers' families always had enough to eat but money for goods which had to be purchased was always a problem. Apart from clothes and boots, money had to be found for flour, tea, salt for pickling, sugar, lamp oil or candles, school books. These were the domestic wants, but money was also needed to buy farm supplies, such as seeds for oats and vegetables. Finding the money for rates and Land Commission annuities was also difficult, though the annuities were considered cheap compared to the rents payable to the landlords.

Until the decline of the fishing industry in the 1930s most farmers were fishermen as well, giving rise to the oft-quoted remark that "when the men fished most of the farming work fell on the women".

Mrs O'Shea of Coarhabeg is now over 80 but is well able to describe conditions in her youth and to confirm that these did not differ very much from her mother's time. She got up at 7.30 a.m. and earlier after the Creamery came. You cleaned out the open turf fire and put fresh sods on the ashes called in Irish the "griosach". You had to wait for the kettle to boil. Then you made porridge or prepared bread and milk for the children. When the children had departed to school, you cleaned up and started on your out-door work. First you milked the cows; then you strained the milk. In winter, you fed the calves, having boiled the porridge on the open fire in large heavy pots which had to be swung into place. The hens were fed next but they got all the scraps and a pot of potatoes with meal and oats. Eggs were always sold in the village shop until the creamery came and the egg-money, like the turkey money at Christmas, was the housewives' personal income. When asked if this gave the wife a certain independence Mrs O'Shea drolly replied that "the farmer's wife had the spending of the egg money but the husband and children had the eating of it too". At the beginning of this century a very thrifty, hardworking wife would be able to pay for all her basic weekly groceries for a large family from the egg money and have enough left over for a pound of Denny's rashers and sausages or a large packet of plain biscuits. .

The dinner was early and consisted normally of potatoes and fish. Mrs O'Shea complained that the men "never made a shape" to come in time for their dinner, so that the wife had great difficulty in keeping it hot, all on an open fire, and where other pots had to be boiled. The dinner dishes had to be washed up next. The man of the house might fall asleep in the chair for an hour after his dinner but the women never had time for such a luxury. If a young wife was caught by her mother-in-law having a stolen nap on the "Rack" or settle in the kitchen, she would get a proper scolding.

Afternoon meant that the cows had to be milked again and the calves fed again and more potatoes boiled. In the early days there was no pump and all water had to be drawn from your own well. If there was a good summer Valentia suffered from the same difficulty as the rest of rural Ireland. Some wells went dry and on really bad years you might have to catch and tackle the ass and car and travel a mile to another well and this could continue from March to the end of September. When you got there you might be unlucky enough to find a queue of people in front of you. If you hadn't an agreeable mother-in-law or sister you might have the additional difficulty of taking small children with you. No houses had running water inside and a very few fortunate farms had gravity-feed water near the house. Practically all farms had a well but the cottiers, or landless men had not.

Needless to say there were no indoor toilets but even in Mrs O'Shea's childhood there was an outside lavatory; this was a dry one necessitating the late evening chore of taking the bucket down to the tide to empty it. Visitors to the island who called to cottages looking for a toilet might get the sort of reply given by Mary Geo, who was very ribald: "Go round the back to the strand and bare your arse to the bairneach's (limpets) like the rest of us."

In the previous century the very poor cottages had dung heaps for both animals and humans directly outside the entrance door.

Mrs O'Shea's description of her daily chores did not include the extra ones. Butter had to be made from the milk; using a dash churn where a paddle had to be pumped up and down, was hard work. The drawing of the dairy maid at Glanleam made about 1850 shows the girl with her churn. A later design of churn involved turning a handle which was less onerous. This wasn't the only work involved; the dishes in which the milk had been set had all to be scrubbed, cleaned and scalded with boiling water from the kettle on the open fire and the finished butter packed into firkins for transporting to the market in Cahirciveen. This involved a journey to Knightstown, then on the ferry where there was a transport charge, and before the coming of the railway, the long haul to Cahirciveen. The butter-merchants had a bore for running into the firkin so that they could test the quality at the bottom as well as what showed on top.

Another factor which affected women's daily lives was the potato crop. Potatoes were a large part of the daily diet. The periods after the crop was starting to rot and before the new potatoes came in, were specially difficult times for the farming wives. They had to produce enough cash to buy meal in the shops and they had to turn this into huge quantities of bread to feed a large family. This was the time when "the women were killed baking". A ten stone bag of flour was normally bought and where there were eight in the house this would last two weeks. A treat was "stampy", potato cakes made with grated raw potatoes. Another variation on the routine food was made in the spring when the new cabbage was coming in. The top leaves of the plants could be picked without spoiling the head. They were boiled to serve with potatoes and fried onions, with about half a pound of butter. When Mrs O'Shea was questioned on the extravagance of using so much butter, she pointed out that the butter was your own and so cost nothing. If you sold it you'd only get 3 1/2d a lb. It was hardly worth selling it when the family needed it.

Other treats in the daily menu were wild rabbit baked in an oven-pot with bacon, and of course there was always fish, fresh, salted or smoked, depending on the supply and the season. Sometimes a pig was killed and salted and the innards were made into black or white puddings. As there was no way of preserving them, these would be shared out among family or neighbours if there was more than could be consumed in the household.

Early in the last century, before the Great Famine, when potatoes and salt, and a little milk were the principal food of the peasantry on Valentia, "they ate some fish, but they sell their eggs. If a wife gives eggs to her family she boasts of it. Two meals a day was usual for labourers when working, as well as when unemployed". This was the diet of a labourer of whom there were 206 on Valentia in 1836 who "laboured for their hire" but only 100 were regularly employed. 150 men were employed at the Slate Quarry then, according to Rev. Day, the Church of Ireland clergyman and he considered people's clothing to be "in general comfortable". He also stated that most labourers had some small amount of land which they cultivated for their own use.

Women who "married in" to farms often had to live with their in-laws. Most houses had some relatives living in them when the new wife moved in but she accepted this because it was the custom of the time and because she knew that the kitchen would be her's when the old people passed on. If the farm had space and there was a little spare money, a small house might be built for the old couple when the first child arrived. These houses had a spacious kitchen downstairs and a bedroom at the top of an open staircase, and sometimes a small bedroom off the kitchen. Except that there was no bathroom, it would have provided as much living-space as a small modern apartment.

Spring and harvest were especially busy times and the women worked in the fields with the men. Turf also had to be cut and saved but it was a cheap fuel and no part of the island was distant from a bog. Labourers on Valentia were considered to be better off than their counterparts in the rich farming areas of Tipperary because they had cheap fuel and fish.

Most of the work was on a "Meitheal" system, groups of neighbours coming together to help one another. But these were also times of fun and community rejoicing and there were often dances in the houses to celebrate the harvest. Cross-roads dancing on Sunday was a very important social occasion. You danced all afternoon, usually on the platform at the top of Bachelor's; home to milk the cows and eat your tea, followed by another dancing session. But the parish priest did not approve and put a stop to it. The clergy also disapproved of the "house dances", sometimes called "porter dances". Perhaps they were alert to the fact that too many very young marriages would produce more children than the country would support after the Great Famine.

Providing clothes for a large family was always a problem but many women were handy with the needle. In the nineteenth century, most clothes were made at home. The women could spin the wool sheared from their own sheep, and it was then knit into jerseys. A child's task was to hold a rush light to provide enough light for the women to spin. The wool was sent to a mill at Ballymalis or to Cork to be spun or woven into cloth. John O'Donoghue remembers a child in the National School in the 1920s having a new jersey admired by the teacher and proudly proffering the information that her granny "carded it, spinned it and knitted it as well. She sheared it too." A few elderly women were making all the jerseys for their grandchildren as late as the 1950s but they were no longer made from their own wool. Often the women made up the patterns as they went along but some women were experts and are remembered by Nora O'Sullivan as being very skilled. Some of this expertise may have come from the knitting industry set up by the women of the FitzGerald family but skills were also acquired in the National Schools. Mrs Barbara Jolley, nee O'Sullivan, an excellent teacher at Knightstown, is remembered as teaching painting, French, embroidery and cooking as well as dancing and crochet.

As well as jerseys for the family women were even known to knit entire suits for their menfolk, and one woman, Biddy Coffey, knit full time for the household in Glanleam.

The bags in which flour and meal came were made of coarse cotton and were carefully hoarded. They could be made into pinafores for the children or they made excellent pillowcases or tea-towels. They could even be stitched together to make sheets. Crochet borders could be put on the children's pinafores and one woman, Babe Shea, had curtains of "bageen" (made from bags) and home-made lace which she used for wakes.

Often clothes were made for children from old clothes or "cast offs" and parcels from America were always a great help, though sometimes of an unsuitable material. Garments were dyed at home. Older women alive today remember that "Diamond" dyes were very successful but these had to be bought in a shop. Earlier home-grown dyes were made from lichens and loosestrife; also a particular "black water" got from a well at Craugh in Cool West; used too, were onion skins for yellows. Earlier, in the eighteenth century, madder was grown on the island. It would appear from the accounts in the papers in Trinity College Library that madder may even have been exported from the island.

Most underclothes were made at home. A bale of cotton or flannelette would be purchased in Cahirciveen, usually after the harvest, or when a pig had been sold. Simple "shifts" were made by the housewife but shirts were often made by an expert. Even as late as 1901 there were several shirt-makers on the island.

Mrs O'Shea described that it was sometimes necessary to stay up until four o'clock in the morning to finish a jersey or to make trousers. The men could not, in her opinion, carry on as long as the women, they were not as "criocnuil" to use her own phrase. This seems rather a harsh judgement when we remember the hours spent rowing a seine or four-oar boat.

Matches were made for the island girls even as late as the 1920s. Sometimes brides came from outside the island. A girl "marrying in" to Feaghmaan in the early years of this century was very pleased to find that she was coming to better living conditions than her family had in

Ballinskelligs. She was especially impressed with the "fine two-storey slated house" she was coming to.

Families on the island, as elsewhere, were large so one wonders how women helped support these. In the last century there were probably better prospects in Valentia than in other areas of the west but there was never enough paid employment for all the women so there was high emigration.

The greatest number of women were in domestic service; the houses built for the staff of the Cable Company in Knightstown were all large Victorian and Edwardian buildings designed to hold large families and capable of being kept very well because domestic labour was both cheap and plentiful. Up to 50 girls worked as maids in Knightstown in the years just after the first World War, at the time when the Cable Station was at its busiest. Apart from the Cable houses, other houses had a resident servant as well as casual help. According to the 1901 Census, the veterinary surgeon and farmer John D. Bremner had two domestics, Julia and Mary McCrohan. Elizabeth Phibbs in Farranreagh had a large staff, Annie Leary, a 20-year-old "nurse domestic-servant" from Dublin, Annie Feeney a 23-year-old house parlour-maid from Sligo and the cook, Mary Cournane, who was from Kerry.

John O'Sullivan, the general merchant in Knightstown, had a large household. He was a widower in 1901 when his two sons, John and Thomas and his two daughters, Lizzie and Bridie were all shop assistants. There were also two granddaughters May and Nellie Baker, two general servants, Norah and Hannah Neill and a 45-year-old baker, Michael O'Sullivan. The next house listed had even more diversified occupations. Julia Hanafin was a very young manageress of a provision store at age 21; there was a general servant, Mary Riordan, a gardener and domestic servant, John Riordan, a baker, Jeremiah Moran, a shop-messenger and servant named Con Fitzpatrick and a bottling man, John Donnelly. Another large establishment was kept by Alexander O'Driscoll who was a coal and timber merchant, a fish dealer, and generally an entrepreneur. His house at Coombe Bank was built to accommodate his large family and there the staff included a governess. Alex's father, "Lord John" had been agent to the Knight of Kerry and as the family prospered they acquired both land and commercial property around Knightstown. When the house at Coombe Bank was being built, the local wits declared that O'Driscolls were building three storeys because they wanted to have the highest house on the island, one storey higher than the Knight's house at Glanleam.

Coombe Bank - the highest house on the island, the home of Alexander O'Driscoll.

A few of the larger farms on the island, especially on the good land in the centre, had resident maids. One wife who had recently acquired such a luxury was sitting in her garden to show the neighbours that she did not need to work. In case they were not sufficiently impressed she is supposed to have shouted "Bridie, baste the goose", to prove that she had a goose in the oven and a Bridie in the kitchen to cook it.

There were numerous "farm servants", girls who worked outdoors on the larger farms. Other occupations included that of Bridget Shea of Dohilla, who, aged a mere 15, was a dressmaker. In Feaghmaan West there were several wool spinners, Johanna Connell, who was 70, and her daughter of the same name. In Ballymanagh, Katie Reidy aged 24 was also a dressmaker but Johanna Kelly in Coarhabeg was a specialist, because she was a shirtmaker. These last girls were all single but one of the wives gave a separate occupation. She was Norah Donoghue from the same townland, a shirtmaker. Other townlands had their share of knitters and sewers but these were not the only occupations. Tinnies Lower East had an egg dealer, Kate Shea, who was 80 and could neither read nor write; Bridget O'Sullivan was a shop assistant and Margaret Devane was a quilt maker; Ellie Jones was the postmistress. In Coarhamore, two girls must have considered themselves different from the other farmers daughters; Ellen O'Connor and her sister Bridget aged 30 and 28, described themselves as "dairy girl to her father" and "milkmaid to her father". They were both single but seem to have occupied a house of their own. Other occupations were washerwoman, housekeeper, governess, the matron at the hospital and the staff at the hotel. In addition to the occupations listed above, there were the standard ones of rural Ireland, the teachers and the postmistress.

The Royal Hotel was always a source of jobs. Outsiders also came to work in the hotel and were often the choice of local men as wives. The hospital also provided employment and attracted new-comers who often married on the island. The hotel always had a good name. Travellers who visited left glowing accounts. For example, Harriet Martineau commended the owner, an Englishwoman who had kept the Hotel for 19 years:

When a window is broken she has the glazier over to mend it. There are no holes in the floor, nor stains of damp on the walls. The carpets, carefully mended, are so bright that you can see there is no dust in them. The forks and spoons shine. The white bed-curtains would show every speck; but there are no specks to show. There is not even a cob-web anywhere; and this is the first time we have missed cob-webs in an Irish Inn. The kitchen is as clean as the bedrooms. We questioned the sensible old lady closely as to how she managed to get her house kept in this way, for she could not if she were half her age, do all this work herself. She told us that she had taken the most likely girls into her service, shown them how she chose to have things done, seen that they were done properly; and if she met with resistance or laziness, sent away the recusant in a thrice.... She cannot keep her servants. However short a time the girls remain with her, they become superior to other girls in their domestic habits, so that they are sought by the men at the Slate Works. The superiority is in most cases still very small; and there is often a sad falling back after a little while, yet their destiny as wives of the most prosperous men on the island, shows what would be the effect of an improved training for women.

During World War I there were additional opportunities for women. Ellie O'Driscoll in Feaghmaan, had a poultry station for hens and ducks and E. Murphy had a similar station for turkeys in Ballyhearny.

Perhaps the strangest job held by any woman was that of help to the wife of the lighthouse keeper on the Skellig Rock, where the families resided with the men until the building of the Lightkeepers' dwellings in Knightstown in 1901. The girl who took this job had to undertake to serve for nine months, presumably to be sure that there would be some female help during the birth of any children. She would have to be companion, housemaid, teacher and mid-wife combined. The sad deaths of two young children on the Skelligs is recorded on the tiny cross which commemorates them in the monk's cemetery there. The last girl to serve on the Skelligs, Joanie Cahill, married in Portmagee and died at a great age some time in the 1950s.

In the middle of the last century, there was considerable discrimination against widows of tenant farmers. Tradition tells that the Knight would not allow a woman to remain as tenant on a farm after her husband's death. She would have had great difficulty in making enough money to pay the rent.

John O'Donoghue tells that his grand-uncle, who was one of the Knight's tenants in Feaghmaan, died. It was usual to offer the farm to a member of the same family. John's grandfather then occupied a smaller farm at the Glebe, near the ruined Church of Ireland. The Knight asked him "Ar mhaith leat dul go Feaghmaan?" (Would you like to go to Feaghmaan"?). He replied "Nil rud ar domhain ab bhearr liom na dul go Feaghmaan" (There is nothing in the world I would like better than to go to Feaghmaan).

The dispossessed wife and family usually got some sort of a "bothan" in the area and would be helped financially and with food by the rest of the family, but widows would have had a very thin time.

Later, when negotiations for the sale of the island to the Congested Districts Board took place, quite a number of women tenants were listed. None of the large farms were held by women but it is not clear whether this was because they would not have been able to hold on to large areas or because they were widows of men who did not themselves possess much land.

Another factor which improved women's lives was the advent of the old age pension. Now, when everyone is entitled to some form of state aid if they have no income, it is very difficult to imagine conditions where there was nothing but private or public charity for those who were destitute. Elderly farmers and labourers were very reluctant to hand over farms or cottages to younger members if they could not be sure that they would have a guaranteed place beside the hearth in their last years. Elderly vagrants were very common but the number decreased noticeably after the old age pension came in. Elderly unwanted relatives suddenly became important, being the only people in the house who had a regular, guaranteed cash income. Women were also known to say they could never conceal their age because it was remembered about them that they were born "the year of the old age pension" in much the same way as islanders remembered the year of the seine boat drownings.

When asked if she thought that women's lives were very difficult and if she had a hard life, Mrs O'Shea of Coarhabeg replied that she didn't think so. Everyone had to work hard and you were satisfied that you were getting a home of your own. Old maids were looked down on and it was always more difficult for a bride if she had to move in to a house where there were any unmarried daughters. Norah O'Sullivan, whose father was a teacher, quotes that the only spinsters they were forbidden by him to make fun of were the Misses Delap, the daughters of the Church of Ireland clergyman.

On the death of the Rev. Alexander Delap, in 1906, the Knight of Kerry gave his widow and three unmarried daughters, Constance, Mary and Maude, the use, for their lifetimes, of "Reenellen", the large house in Knightstown. Maude and Constance became interested in the varied life in the seas around Valentia. Without formal education, they collected and carried out research on marine animals, especially plankton.

Maude (1866-1953) was encouraged in her interest in marine biology by E. T. Browne of University College, London and was to provide valuable assistance to him and to other leading marine biologists. By tow-netting, she discovered a number of rare or new species of jellyfish and medusae. In 1935, Professor Stephenson named a new species of sea anemone which Maude discovered -*Edwardsia delapiae*- "for her skill and persistence in collecting rare species are indefatigable".   She also contributed papers on the archaeology of the area to the proceedings of the Royal Irish Academy and supplied much material for Dr. Scully's "Flora of Co. Kerry".

On the island, the Misses Delap are remembered for their charity.

The Misses Delap saving hay with Mrs Dore.

Chapter Ten
The Famine

No account of life in nineteenth century Ireland is complete without a description of the Famine. Fortunately, the official Famine records provide very good information about conditions on Valentia.

Today when we say "famine" in Ireland we mean the Great Famine of 1845-48, but in fact this was the worst of three famines to hit Ireland, and therefore Valentia, in the nineteenth century.

When Ireland suffered a minor famine in 1822, Maurice FitzGerald, then Knight of Kerry, was conscious of the dangers and wrote to the British Government telling them that the potato crop was bad and that famine was probable. Many proprietors were absent and "the secondary class borne down by the depression of the times. The Government must assist or multitudes will perish".

Some of the aid must have reached south-west Kerry because when Thomas Reid, a Member of the Royal College of Surgeons, London and a Surgeon in the Royal Navy, visited the island in 1822 he left a description of the distribution of the "charity provisions imported by the London Committee for the relief of the Irish poor." Valentia was "in proportion to its size better cultivated and more thickly inhabited" than the rest of Kerry but there was still great poverty. 109 affidavits were produced signed by John Spotswood, a magistrate and a leaseholder from the Knight of Kerry and John Warburton, the Church of Ireland rector. Johanna Driscoll, whose family numbered seven, swore that she had to dig her potatoes on the first of July that year "for want of money or credit". This was very serious as the crop would not have reached maturity so early. She had got only "five pottles of charity meal without payment" by the first of August. David Murphy, a labourer, also had to dig his potatoes early and he got no charity except what he paid for. Catherine Connor, alias M'Carthy, had a similar story and she had a family of ten to feed.

The FitzGeralds were involved in the distribution of the charity meal, which was stored at Glanleam. About seven tons were still remaining, although Reid had been assured that it was all spoiled. It had been kept in an upstairs room, but the floor gave way and it was removed to a store room, which being considered unsafe, it was brought back again and deposited in a parlour. Reid also verified that the accounts of the distribution "appeared to be kept with great exactness". Reid concluded that "vast numbers of distressed individuals have had their sufferings alleviated by the distribution of the charitable funds".

All Kerry was in a disturbed state because included in the State Papers for 1822 is an entry that the "Officer commanding Valentia yeomanry has been instructed to communicate with Lord Headly as to accommodation of troops in mountains of Glenbeigh and if procurable to station men there". The Yeomanry were an armed force loyal to the Crown and in this case to the Knight.

In November the same year the Knight, Maurice, was writing from Listowel that Whiteboys had procured gunpowder from Tralee.

Even after the famine of 1822, feeding the growing population of Valentia, like the rest of Ireland, was a major problem. The island population increased and this was the period when employment became available in the slate quarry. Ready money was earned in the quarry and the labourers on the island were better paid than on the mainland, earning from one shilling to two shillings and sixpence a day. This meant greater prosperity but it also resulted in a reduction in the amount of food grown on the island and there was no longer a surplus for export.

Even in 1845 Rev. George Day, the Church of Ireland rector, was aware of approaching famine. With the churchwardens, he made an application for relief stating that there were in the parish "upwards of 100 families without one week's food, or the means of purchasing it; that though the island had been accustomed to supply other parts with potatoes, there was not a single person who had one peck for sale; and that no adequate aid could be afforded by private means." In June of 1846 the people in the entire area were beginning to eat the potatoes set aside for seed for the next year, something that was akin to suicide.

The Knight of Kerry and the magistrates and cesspayers of the district of Valentia sent a memorial dated 2nd May 1846 to the Government stating that "within the last few days, it has been ascertained that the rot in potatoes is frightful, that 200 men have been turned off work by the owners of the slate quarries in the district." They earnestly begged a supply of Indian meal and that a ship be moored in Valentia Harbour, to issue meal for cash payments; that the works recommended by the Co. Surveyor for Valentia were rejected and praying the Government to send an officer to inspect and report on such works, "as may entitle that district to a share of the Government Relief". The crop loss on Valentia was quoted at 1/2.

The Government reply was that it was necessary as a first step that a local relief committee should be formed and that when this was done and subscriptions obtained, the Government would immediately add a donation. If the committee suggested any work at Valentia as employment of the peasantry from the subscriptions, an officer of the Board of Works would be requested to report on such work. The letter also stated that the coastguard officer at Valentia had power to issue free Indian meal in small quantities where it was deemed necessary. There was a note that there was no idle labour on the island.

The Knight also wrote to Lord Russell at Downing St., because on 1st July 1846 Russell replied "It is with some regret I learn that the forthcoming potato crop in Ireland shows symptoms of disease. The measures you suggest in anticipation of this calamity shall have the due consideration of the Government".

Some relief did arrive because a sum of £15 was sent to the rector and churchwardens and three cargoes of potatoes (129 tons) were forwarded to Valentia by Mr. Dombrain, who was the head of the coastguards.

In March 1846 a list of coastguard stations where supplies of Indian corn were available for sale included Valentia, which also served Portmagee. Indian corn was not a very acceptable food to the majority of Irish in distress. The Quaker records show that the recipients did not know how to cook it; they had no ovens to bake it and often were too weak to build up fires to cook it in pots for long periods. Those who ate it raw became ill.

On 20th November 1846 the Knight wrote from Valentia to the Chief Secretary that at a meeting of the magistrates, clergy and gentry, a resolution was passed that supplies of food for the western coast of Ireland should be sent there, direct from America. As Valentia was the nearest Irish port to America it was suggested that a depot vessel be moored there to receive the supplies direct from New York. The memorial also looked for a grant to extend the proposed railway from Killarney to Valentia and for a loan of £6,000 to purchase rye, bere, and barley, to supply seed to farmers, the loan to be secured to the Government by the relief committee of the district. This was to enable them to grow food in place of the potato "which must now be looked upon as a very uncertain crop".

Application for a loan of £6,000 made to the British Government by Maurice FitzGerald, Knight of Kerry, during the time of the Great Famine.

A committee was set up which included Maurice, the Knight of Kerry, John G. Day, the Church of Ireland rector, J. Maginn, the Catholic parish priest, Alex Brock, the post master, and one Blennerhassett, land agent and receiver." They claimed that the public works recommended for Valentia had been discriminated against by the committee in Cahirciveen! Their representations must have been successful because in January of 1847 the Knight and the Rev. Day were asking for the immediate commencement of the works which had been sanctioned for Valentia. These included the opening of the "proposed line of road between Coarhabeg and Cool to Cooskerry". Other works carried out as famine relief on the island were the making of landing places at White Strand, (Glanleam?) for which a grant of £150 was given and at "the end of the road at the old Coast Station" for which £100 was given. In 1847 a fishery station was erected and curing was to be carried on there.

When we realise that many people died from fever and cholera as well as from starvation, the presence on the island of a temporary hospital must have helped. It is believed to have been "Ballyhearny House", the large two-storey house, now derelict, on O'Sullivan's farm, just below the middle road. The hospital is described in an unsigned article in Charles Dickens' "Household Words" in 1852 as follows:

> Besides the cabins and cottages, we saw, near this road, one solitary dreary-looking white house. It was tall and rather large, with no garden or field belonging to it. Its windows looked as if they had never been opened; its woodwork as if it had not been painted for a century; and its whitewash was grey with weather stains. It was the Cholera Hospital.

Presumably the hospital was no longer in use in 1852, the potato famine and the fever being then over.

Older people tell that there was a coffin in one of the upstairs rooms of the house for years after the famine which had a false bottom. Such coffins were common during the famine, the bottom being made so that it could slide out and deposit the corpse into the grave, often a common one. It is said that the coffin was left outside the graveyard so that it could be collected by the next person who needed it.

The official statistics about this hospital are meagre. It had to serve also Caher, Killymaan, Killemanagh and Prior. In May of 1847 a temporary fever hospital and dispensary was established. Medicines suggested for cholera treatment in such hospitals were carbonate of ammonia, 40 grains to be dissolved in 1/2 pint of water and two spoonfuls taken every hour. Other remedies were pills of powdered opium, 1/4 grain each, with 2 grains of powdered ginger made up with oil of peppermint or pills of mercury and opium made up with oil of caraway.

The hospital provided for 15 patients and there were two nurses and one wardsmaid. The Board of Health sanctioned a general scale of payment for its medical officers of 5/- per day and indeed many of them died during the famine. The fever hospital got no grant in aid, so we do not know how it was supported.

Most of the islanders must have received some aid in the form of food. The Government returns show that the maximum number of people supplied with food in any one day was 2,008 out of an entire population of 2,920. Most aid had to be paid for so that an island where 300 men were still employed in the Slate Quarry was at least in the position of having cash flow, the main lack in other areas of the West. The total amount advanced on Valentia by the Relief Commissioners was £586, a lot of money when collected in shillings and pennies.

Stories told about the famine on the island include how the queue of people waiting for food from the Knight of Kerry's house at Glanleam stretched almost as far as Knightstown. This was presumably the soup kitchen on Valentia for which the Quakers supplied the boilers. When the official supply of rations on the island ended in September 1847, 1257 persons were getting daily relief. Food was issued from the soup kitchen at Glanleam after this. The Quaker Relief Organisation continued into 1848 when they supported a soup kitchen dispensing 620 quarts a day in Valentia, "where there was no other help". The cost was quoted as a barrel of meal a day and all contributions had fallen off except the aid given by the Knight of Kerry and grants from the Quaker Committee.

The island benefited from the fact that no part was very remote from Glanleam, unlike areas where the poor had great difficulty getting to soup kitchens and carrying away the stirabout, or where there were no soup kitchens near and even the Workhouse was 30 miles away. A resident landlord and two clergymen were in a position to look for any aid that was available. This was in direct contrast to areas of Connacht where there was no one to form any kind of committee.

Another story is that a grain ship came in to Valentia Harbour and that meal was supplied from it. This may have been the Andromeda which ran aground in the harbour in November or December 1846.

One famine story is related by a Valentia man working in London in the years after World War I. He was returning from working on a late shift. He sheltered from heavy rain and got into conversation with an elderly Kerryman who was very anti-British in his outlook. By way of explanation the old man told that as a child he had been sent by his family to walk from Kenmare to Valentia to collect meal which was being distributed from a ship there. Kenmare was 50 miles away and was very badly hit by the Famine but he was the only one fit to walk such a distance. He recalled two factors.... the nearer he got to Cahirciveen the more corpses there were on the road and that he got only a stone or two of meal or flour and it had weevil in it. There is also a story that on one part of the island the potatoes did not develop the dreaded blight. Could this have been east of Clynacartan village at Foilhomurrum Bay where 65 tons of ore were raised in 1861 containing 22 3/8 % copper and 34 3/4 tons with 24 1/8 copper the following year? Copper is one of the ingredients in the spray which is used today to prevent blight on potatoes.

William Bennett, who spent six weeks in Ireland in 1847, reported about Valentia that :

> the cottages in the interior are poor, and the people undergoing much hardship, but there did not appear to be that intense degree of misery and suffering we had witnessed in some other parts. We spoke to one poor man at work on his plot, inquiring what he was going to set. "Faith, God knows" was his answer "I have nothing at all, at all" .... He had the first patch of potatoes we had seen any-where up; and seeing his industry, we had much pleasure in telling him to prepare all the land he was able to, and apply to the clergyman, or the other gentleman, in a week's time.

The island tradition that it escaped the worst of the Famine may be true and it was accepted by the Society of Friends Historians that no area in Kerry was as bad as Connacht, but it was still a terrible time. Ten years afterwards, when the Trans-Atlantic Cable was landed on the island, a journalist could report that "the island of Valentia suffered fearfully during the Famine in Ireland and hundreds died of starvation on the road side or in the miserable dwellings; their bodies were found many weeks after their deaths, unburied, and in a horrible state of emaciation ."

Conditions in Ireland were never again as bad as in "The Hungry Forties" but the early 1880s were a period of dropping prices for agricultural produce and a partial failure of the potato crop. Conditions on Valentia were made worse by the drop in employment in the Quarry. The late Jeremiah O'Leary of Feaghmaan, when in his eighties, considered that the Knight may have been more far-seeing than the tenants gave him credit for. Payment in cash would have been of little use if there was a repetition of the conditions of the Great Famine and no food to be bought. Carrick, the stone-mason, who reported the meal-payments to the Magnus Company in England, saw no reason to accept meal when he needed cash to purchase a pair of gutta- percha boots to wear in the mine. The company sent someone to investigate the situation and as a result all payments in meal ceased.

Appeals were made for help in the 1880 famine also. The Nun of Kenmare, the controversial Sister M.F. Clare Cusack, sent £30, half the amount given by her to Adrigole and to Kilgarvan. Castletownbere must have been considered the most needy area as it got £80. By this time the population of Valentia had dropped to 2240 so there were fewer mouths to feed. According to Charles Russell, whose "New Views on Ireland" was published in 1880, "about £12,000 passed through the hands of the Relief Committee on Valentia Island, which sum went to assist the tenants of Trinity College and the Knight of Kerry, and I am informed that there were not 20 of these tenants who did not receive relief. So far as I could learn the landlords contributed nothing to the charitable funds, but the Knight of Kerry did supply seed potatoes to some of his tenants, in some instances at market price and in other cases below the market price." The meal and seed potatoes came mostly from the charitable funds subscribed and distributed through the agency of the Duchess of Marlborough's committee, the Mansion House Committee and the Committee of the Land League in Dublin. This must have been one of the numerous occasions when the Valentia tenants benefited by having a resident landlord.

Chapter Eleven
Other Newcomers to Valentia

Early outsiders who came to live on Valentia were the garrison of the two forts erected by Cromwell in 1659 at either end of the island. The first garrison comprised 60 men and four years later the fort had one ensign, two corporals, one drummer, and 33 soldiers, as well as a gunner who was paid 12d per day. But they can hardly have left much impression on the population as the garrison remained only a few years.

The Coastguards

The coastguards were the next outside influence and they were already having their children baptised in the Church of Ireland in 1826. Many of them were members of one or other of the Low Churches but would have had no facilities and so their baptisms and marriages took place in the Church of Ireland. Those recorded include William Cocks of Laharn and his wife Sarah(1828), Edw. and Lydia Pound (1875) and names like Rae, Hawker, Reed, Starke, Ward, and Bickford.

Very often coastguards were ex-British Navy boatmen and came from English sea-ports. One such was James Haffinden who was stationed in Knightstown in 1901. He came from Eastbourne in Sussex and his wife from Norfolk. The coastguards were moved very often. Haffinden's children were born in Weybourne and Hunstanton. The Chief Officer at this period was Charles Geeve, who gave Jersey, Channel Islands as his place of birth; his wife was from Wiltshire but his child was born in Co. Kerry. William Hammans was English with a Canadian wife and children born in Mayo and Donegal. Almost all the coastguards in 1901 were Protestant, either Church of Ireland, Church of England or Wesleyan. By

1911 about half were Catholic and William Young, Bartholomew Flahavin and John Bready were Irish born.

The coastguards seem to have been on reasonably good terms with the local population. The fishermen took them in their boats on fishing trips and gave them part of their catch, often in return for tobacco. Their efforts at potato culture provided local amusement. One man who asked for advice when his potato crop was poor, was discovered to have peeled the seed potatoes before planting. When asked if he had left an "eye" in each "Scollan" or seed section, he replied "Bugger me eyes; I never knew there were eyes in a spud".

Sometimes the children of coastguards intermarried with the local population and there were tales of daughters who ran off with someone's husband. It is also remembered that the wife of one coastguard was a great nurse, better than any doctor.

Coast Guard House at Carriglea. Vacated 1922

Coastguards lived at Laharn in the first half of the nineteenth century and later at Peter St. and in Coastal Terrace in Knightstown. Other houses were built at Carriglea, near where the bridge is now located. A good stone slated house was a concession well worth having with the job, though the coastguard houses were smaller than Cable or lighthousekeepers accommodation and there were no bathrooms or running water. A pump was provided in the yard for each set of houses.

After the State was set up in 1922 one man stayed on in the Carriglea houses for some time but the houses then became derelict. The Coastal Terrace in Knightstown provided accommodation for the Garda's families; some houses were converted to a youth hostel and others became private accommodation.

Daniel Jenkins, Captain of the Coastguard.

The Valentia Meteorological Station.

Valentia Meteorological Station owes its beginnings to the observations begun on the island as far back as 1860 when the system of

120

weather telegraphy was introduced by Admiral Fitzroy. The work was undertaken by R. J. Lecky, the manager of the Quarry and the first report issued was for 8.a.m. on 8th October 1860. These reports continued until 1867, when the Meteorological Committee of the Royal Society decided to establish an Observatory on the island. The Observatory (now demolished) also had to serve as a residence for the Superintendent. The first Superintendent was Rev. Kerr. He died suddenly in 1872 and was buried on Valentia. His successor was J.E. Cullum who had previously been magnetic assistant at the station at Kew. He was responsible for the establishment of a Magnetic Observatory at Kilbeg known as "Cullum's Cup".

From the outset, it had been planned to develop Valentia Observatory, not only as a climatological observatory but also as a geophysical one. Absolute observations of the earth's magnetic field were begun in 1888.

The Meteorological Station, since demolished.

The house on Valentia became too small for the observatory and the residence of the Superintendent. A more suitable site for the observatory could not be purchased on the island. As a result the observatory transferred to Cahirciveen in 1892 but retained its original title thus making Valentia a household name.

The Wireless Station.

When the island lost the Observatory it gained another institution. The first Wireless Station was established by Marconi at Reenadrolaun Point (the Wren's Point), thereafter called also the "Wireless Point". Even the building of the permanent house provided employment.

The station was taken over in 1909 by the British Post Office and until 1921 was manned by Royal Navy personnel. From that time until 1950, it was operated on a contract basis by the Irish Post Office for the British Post Office. Since then the station has been run by various Irish Government departments.

Today, Valentia Radio Station broadcasts weather bulletins and forecasts, gale and navigation warnings, and provides telephone and telegraph service to and from ships, trawlers, oil rigs, survey vessels and pleasure craft. Its most important function is to save lives at sea. A continuous 24-hour watch is maintained on the international distress frequencies and the station is in contact with the Marine Rescue Co-ordinating Centre at Shannon and with lifeboat and coast life saving services.

The early Radio Station.

Houses were built in the village of Knightstown to accommodate the staff, though like the Cable staff the Wireless staff never had enough houses to go round. When men with local connections joined the service many built attractive individual houses throughout the island.

The Wireless staff, like the Lightkeepers, were never as numerous as the Cable staff but contributed considerably to the island's economy. Because they were part of the world of communications, islanders trained as radio officers for work all over the world, some returning to become part of the staff on their own island.

The Lighthouse Keepers

In 1901 another group of outsiders was added to the island's permanent population.

The island had its own lighthouse with a residence at Cromwell Point since 1841. It had been applied for in 1828 by Maurice FitzGerald, the Knight of Kerry, and by Maurice O'Connell in 1837. The light was "exhibited" a year before the lighthouse and the compound were completed and the cost at the end of 1842 was £10, 846.17.11, a staggering sum at that time.

In 1901 Trinity House in London, which controlled the Lighthouse Service, built the block of eight houses on the edge of Knightstown, known locally as the "lightkeepers' dwellings". Up to this time the families of the keepers lived with their men on the remote Rock Stations, like Skellig and Tighreacht. The corner houses were the residences of the principal keepers of the Skellig and the Tighreacht lighthouses and the other six houses were for the staff, one being for the unmarried keepers.

The wives of the keepers had the loneliest life of any islanders because their husbands were on duty and away from home for six weeks out of every eight in normal weather but this could extend if the boat was unable to land to take off the keepers. Leo Jones, a serving lightkeeper, was the third generation to serve "in the Lights". In the 39 years of service his father had spent only 5 Christmases at home.

If the husband was to remain on the Rock over Christmas, the wives "would be killed baking and sending goodies". They took a very poor view of accounts in the newspapers which implied that the extra supplies came from the Commissioners of Irish Lights.

At the time when the "shore dwellings" at Valentia were built four keepers were attached to each of the stations, Skellig and Tighreaght, a principal keeper, and three assistants. Reliefs, or changes of personnel, were carried out every two weeks and keepers did six weeks on and two off. The keeper off duty lived at the shore dwellings and had various duties to perform while there. It wasn't until the 1970s that the Rock Stations became manned by six keepers with resulting shorter tours of duty.

The day when the change-over of duties took place was one of great tension. Watching the weather to see if the boat could land was a source of anxiety and if the men could not get away, there was the same difficulty each day until the weather changed. The men had to be down at the pier every morning during the "Relief Period".

The keepers had to bring with them on duty food supplies to last six weeks and clothes and bedding. It was often commented that only women with long experience could possibly pack so much into such a small container. Most of the men were good cooks and could bake their own bread. They also kept goats for milk and could fish from the rocks to supplement their supplies. There was always the danger they might run out of food or tobacco. Mrs Sheila Keenan, a light-keeper's wife, emphasised the importance of being a good cook, because when the men came off duty after cooking for themselves, they appreciated a wife's good food.

Wives who came from Valentia and married Lightkeepers were more fortunate than strangers. When the husband was away her mother would send one of the younger sisters or brothers to stay with the young wife. This was appreciated, especially when the first baby arrived.

The Lightkeepers were subject to a strict set of rules about visitors. They were not allowed to keep paying guests and permission had to be obtained from head office to have relations to stay.

Like Cable staff, the keepers got very good houses, rent free and various perks, such as six tons of free coal per year and a year's supply of paraffin. Because they were moved from one lighthouse to another, the family were provided with much of their basic household equipment; beds and other basic furniture were supplied and even pots and pans.

In the early days, the houses had an underground water tank which collected water from all the roofs and one man's duty was to pump this daily. There were also huge stone tanks in each yard which were reputed to store 2,000 gallons of water, giving rise to the fact remembered by older people that "the lightkeepers had water even when it was scarce."

The houses were maintained to a very high standard by the Commissioners of Irish Lights. They were regularly painted inside and out and the gravel around the houses had to be renewed and kept free from weeds. There was even a flag pole in the grounds and the flag was lowered at sunset.

There were periodic inspections of the station which were very traumatic in the early days. The inspector was even known to turn back the bed-clothes or run his finger along the top of a door to check that there was no dust. Wives with large families or those who were poor housekeepers got help from the other families to prepare for the dreaded inspections.

The Census of 1911, which listed where people were born, showed that the Lightkeepers children were born all over Ireland. Richard Isaac Wright, the principal keeper of the lighthouse on Valentia, had children born in Counties Down, Clare, Wexford, Wicklow, and Kerry.

The families who served in the Irish Lights were often related and several generations followed one another in the service, resulting in a small close-knit society. This may have not always been appreciated by the wives but it meant that help was available when needed, very important in a community where three quarters of the men were absent all the time.

The greatest difficulty for the wives was that they had to deal with all the day-to-day problems; you could not wait six weeks for the husbands to come back. The only communication from the husband was a letter once a fortnight when the relief boat came in. All the emergencies had to be dealt with including illness and child-birth. The houses were available to the staff only until the men were 60 and after that they had to buy houses or get alternate accommodation.

A Lightkeepers job was considered worth having, particularily in the 1930s. When the houses were all occupied there was considerable socialising between the families and local people; many keepers married local girls. Tales have survived of great card games and even dances in the large comfortable living room with its dresser and range.

The keepers had secure employment and their cheque came every month. If a husband did not let his wife cash the cheque, she was dependent on buying goods "on tick" but everybody bought goods on credit then anyhow. Perhaps these were the wives who were "delighted to see the back of him" when the husband departed on duty. In some respects too, the father was a stranger to the children.

The dwellings with their four acres were sold by Irish Lights in 1965 and after that the keepers provided their own accommodation.

Living on a compound and with two thirds of the menfolk away all the time must have produced difficulties.

When the men were on shore duty there were various maintenance tasks to be carried out. A log of what they did each day had to be filled in. Entries of "private business" in Cahirciveen occurred regularly. When one of today's Lightkeepers was asked what these visits could possible have been, he suggested that these were days spent in the public houses in Cahirciveen.

Whatever the difficulties of life in the dwellings for Lightkeepers' families, the older wives must have considered these houses real luxury after the hardship of living on the Skellig Rock or the Tighreacht, the lighthouse beyond the Blasket Islands. Life on the edge of a village, with schools, and churches, both Catholic and Protestant, an hotel, shops, a post office and a hospital was luxury compared to life for the family on the Rock.

The eight houses for the families of the Lighthouse keepers built in 1901.

Chapter Twelve
Island Amenities and Sports.

The first post office was established on Valentia in 1820 and its first postmark was Valentia/176, the number being the distance from Dublin in Irish miles. The postmaster from 1844-53 was Alexander Brock and he was succeeded by Thomas Young in 1855. The Young family probably built the first hotel in Knightstown.

The first recorded school on Valentia was erected when Robert FitzGerald, the 17th Knight of Kerry, obtained a grant from the governors of the Erasmus Smith Schools in 1776 "towards building an English school".

The Erasmus Smith Foundation was set up in 1657 to "bring up the youth (of Ireland) to be principlined in literature and good manners" but its schools were generally regarded as proselytising. Robert FitzGerald was a member of the board of governors and was therefore in a good position to persuade the board to use part of its funds for Valentia. An allocation had been made to provide two schools "in some remote part of this Kingdom".

The first master of the Erasmus Smith school at Zelva was Joseph Smith at a salary of £20 per annum. In its first ten years the school never had more than 48 pupils. Smith is reported to have scrupulously refrained from any appearance of proselytising and was therefore unpopular with the Protestant clergyman.

In 1788 a new school house was built by Smith. The first master there was a man named Ball after whom the area was called, Ball's Heights. The substantial two-story ruin of the Erasmus Smith school in Kilbeg townland near O'Driscoll's farm is still visible today. The building was later used as a school by the Irish Island and Coast Society, another

Protestant foundation. It is shown on a FitzGerald map of 1851 as the "Hibernian Society school." At all stages it seems to have had few pupils. In 1871 it had 29 Catholic pupils, four Protestants and three "Presbyterians and other".

After Ball the next teacher was McCarthy and after him John McKew, an Aran islander and native Irish speaker, was selected to take charge of the school. John McKew and his wife Anne lived on into this century. Mrs McKew is very kindly remembered by Norah O'Sullivan, who often called in to McKew's house on her way home from school. A second Protestant National School was later built in Knightstown.

The Catholic church in Chapeltown was the location of the next recorded school. About 1831, 180 boys and 45 girls attended there, all but 21 being Catholics. Both versions of the bible were read, presumably to accommodate the Protestant Episcopalians. It was a pay school and the Master was James Burke. A second school was kept by Timothy O'Driscoll, where 168 boys and 40 girls were taught reading, writing and arithmetic, for which the parents paid. A third school was subsidised by the Knight of Kerry and the Protestant rector. It was a free school teaching the "three R's" and the Master was James Donohue. These schools were sometimes referred to as "hedge schools".

The parish priest, Father McGinn, was so anxious to get a National School for the island that he had actually built the schoolhouse at Ballyhearny, near Chapeltown, before writing to the Board of Education in 1842 for aid for salary and books. The teacher was Patrick Donohue and as in all National Schools the instruction and the text books were English. The P.P. quoted that the books used were "Voster's Arithmetic, Jackson's Bookkeeping, Murray's Grammar, Dillon's Spelling Book and many different histories"; he was also making sure that the Board knew that "the school is kept under my management".

The schools at Knightstown and Coarhabeg were built later and survived until the new school was built in Chapeltown a few years ago. In the 1920s a small private school was opened in Knightstown and was used mainly by children from the Cable station. The Knight of Kerry's children always had tutors and governesses and so did the family of Alexander O'Driscoll, the local merchant and entrepreneur.

As all National Schools taught English only, the Irish speakers on the island did not learn to read or write their native language until the beginning of this century. Dan O'Sullivan, the teacher, held Irish classes at that time but they had to take place after school hours. School attendance did not become compulsory until early this century, which accounts for the number on the island who could neither read nor write English -- 730 men and 1110 women in 1841. Fifty years later the number had dropped to 261 men and 381 women. As the Census forms did not ask who could read or write Irish, we have no information on literacy in the islander's native language.

The island had both Catholic and Protestant Churches from very early times. Before the Slate Quarry was opened and Knightstown built and prior to the building of the Cable station, the south west part of the island was the most populated and its centre was Chapeltown. The mill was situated there and the very early Catholic church. The ruins of an older church were visible in the grave yard in 1837 and there may have been other churches or houses where Mass was celebrated. The present church in Chapeltown was built just over 50 years ago to replace the older structure. The old church had no seats for many years so that the older women "lucht na seal" (the women in shawls) brought their stools with them to Mass but sat with their backs to the altar. Tomas O'Criomthain in "An t-Oileanach" left a description of the congregation:

> When the congregation was collected they were all very neatly dressed, and though it was an island you would have thought that they had been brought up in the centre of the country. And as for clean, respectable clothes, those were the sort they wore. When we went into the chapel, the central part of it was open up to the rafters, while the rest of it was covered with a loft on the inside of each gable. Whether I said few or many prayers, they didn't prevent me from casting an eye on the congregation, and I didn't see a swarthy skin or a black-haired head among them in the chapel or out.

The church in Knightstown was not built until 1913. The removal of the main church to Knightstown was very controversial but by this time the centre of activity had largely shifted to that side of the island. The house for the parish priest had already been built there.

In the days when there was only one church and one Mass on Sundays and holidays, everyone could not get to Mass. Someone had to stay at home to mind very young children. The island was better served for churches even before the Knightstown church was built because Chapeltown was central. In other areas people had to walk over the mountains to Mass and they went fasting. Brother Peter Lynch remembers that when he was a small child going to Mass in Chapeltown all the older people spoke Irish between themselves. Irish remained the daily language of those who lived "back the island" long after English was spoken around Knightstown.

The Church of Ireland community was very well served for such a small area. Today islanders associate the Protestant church with the staff of the Cable Station, but the island had a Protestant church which was reported in ruins in 1775 and a Glebe House. The ruined church beside the grave yard dates from 1815 and had 56 acres attached to the Glebe. The present church in Knightstown was built about 1885.

The island had a number of Protestant farmers and labourers as well as some tradesmen like Thomas Shuel, a mason in 1828, Henry Ware, a sawyer and Thomas Carter, a nailor (1835). These were probably some of the Welsh miners brought in to teach the local population skills at the Quarry. They may not have originally been Church of England. Coastguards also helped to increase the Church of Ireland congregation. Children of the Lightkeepers on the island and one child from the Skellig Rock, were baptised in the island church.

The family of Bewicke Blackburn, the manager of the Quarry, were Protestant and they even brought their servants with them. "Gentlemen" like Frances Chute in 1846, and Robert Bell in 1849; farmers like Jeffcott Smith, (1846) presumably one the Smiths of Donnybrook, once known as "Caol Smith"; shop-keepers like John Brock who was also the postmaster; doctors, engineers such as Vitus Merrick (1848); land agents like Captain Needham of Trinity College, and various officials like the teachers in the Protestant schools, the Lightkeepers, the Coast Guards, and the policemen all combined to form the local Protestant community.

Of course the Knight of Kerry and his family were also an important part of the Church of Ireland congregation and most of the FitzGeralds are buried in the island Protestant Graveyard. Many of the

Glanleam staff were also Church of Ireland like Robert Hallett, the gardener, whose son Ethelred Charles was baptised in 1900.

The arrival of the Trans-Atlantic Cable was the biggest single impetus into the Church of Ireland on Valentia. Many of the staff were Episcopalians and Methodists but attended the only Church available to them. Once local men were taken on at the Cable Station there was considerable inter-marrying with the island population resulting in a number of mixed marriages. These never seemed to cause any friction and the 1901 Census shows several Protestant men with Catholic wives and a smaller number of Catholic men with Protestant wives. It also showed a wide variety of members of other sects including Lady FitzGerald who was Jewish.

A major addition to the island was its hotel. Its earliest recorded owner was Mrs Young. The various royal visits helped to enhance its reputation and the amenities put in for these visits were very advanced at the time.

Of more importance to most islanders was the hospital. The original wooden building provided for the Cable Company at Foilhomurrum was no longer needed on the completion of the station at Knightstown in 1871. The post office presented the redundant Cable hut to the people of Valentia. It was re-sited just outside Knightstown on a site given by the Knight of Kerry and became the hospital. The early hospital had accommodation for 14 patients and it was possible to divide off part of the building for infectious cases. The trustees of the hospital were the Catholic and Church of Ireland clergymen of the island and they were assisted by a voluntary committee. The FitzGerald family served in several capacities and the committee included at various times, Captain Needham, the Trinity College agent, the wife of the doctor, the director of the Observatory, members of the Driscoll family and later the daughters of Rev. Delap, the Church of Ireland Clergyman, T. Galvin, who owned the Hotel and a number of the staff of the Cable Station including Mrs D. O'Sullivan, who was also involved in the Women's National Health Association.

The hospital was intended to cater for the poor of the island and was self-supporting. Patients were expected to pay something towards expenses if they could afford it and very often they paid in kind. In 1909, one patient's bill amounted to 6.6. She contributed "181 pints of milk and 13 doz eggs which left a balance of 4s/9d1/2 to be paid.

The hospital was to serve, primarily, the people of the dispensary district of Valentia and Portmagee but it also served many others. In 1872 three seamen were admitted and two in each of the years 1907-8 and 1908-9. Throughout the nineteenth century, Valentia harbour was a hive of activity. Besides the many trading and fishing boats, there were Royal Navy patrols, Cable and Irish Lights ships calling and the crews of these boats were often glad to avail of the hospital services. Other patients were jobbing workmen and "vagrants". There was also the difficulty about paying and non-paying patients and the busy Matron had to serve as District Nurse as well. In the early days she travelled in a donkey and car but about 1910 the donkey was "laid up" and it was decided to wait to see how Nurse Hickson "got on with the bicycle" before arranging to get a new donkey.

When Lady FitzGerald obtained the Tallerman Treatment of rheumatism and arthritis for the hospital, people came from quite far away to try it. After two additions had been put on to the early building, the wooden hut became a fever unit. The hospital was never large but it served the local community well. Few rural areas had a local hospital and it enabled islanders to be treated near home. Sometimes there was a divergence of opinion whether or not advanced cases of tuberculosis should be treated or sent to the Workhouse at Cahirciveen. Today, we are inclined to forget that typhus and typhoid were endemic in the west of Ireland but the records show that both of these conditions were treated. On the night the 1901 Census was taken there were four patients in the hospital, an English seaman with a fractured clavicle, the result of a fall, a 60-year-old Kerry widower with bronchitis; the captain of a barque from Norway, who had rheumatic fever, and a 6 year old girl with typhoid fever. Minor surgery was carried out at the hospital, even a breast was removed as well as an appendix and glands.

World War I was a busy period. Military were stationed by the British Government on the island to ensure the safety of the Cable and Wireless Stations and Navy personnel manned the look- out post on Bray Head. Men from the British Navy ships *Safeguard*, *Drake* and others were regularly treated for shipboard injuries and bronchitis. The large number of men from the York, and Lancaster Regiments and Royal Dublin and

Royal Irish Fusiliers who were encamped in the Sports Field near the Cable Station may not have suffered from the ills of active service but they were treated for influenza, bronchitis, laryngitis, rheumatic fever and pneumonia for which the army paid the hospital the sum of 3/- per patient per day. Later, when the State was set up, the hospital was "practically taken over by the Free State Troops" and here again the new Republic recompensed the hospital for its service.

Perhaps the best tribute to the hospital was paid by Peter Delap, one of the grand-children of Rev. Delap, the Church of Ireland clergyman. When he visited there as a medical student in the 1930s he was shown round by his aunt, Miss Mary Delap and voiced his opinion that such a barely equipped establishment was no hospital. A decade later, he was unfortunate enough to get extensively wounded during a Commando operation in Albania. On returning to the comparative safety of Italy he realised, literally in his bones, how much it must have meant to injured sailors landed at Valentia to be warm and dry and at rest, with decent food.

Today, the hospital is still serving the local community and many visitors have been very glad to avail of its services for minor burns and accidents. Another addition to Knightstown was the Fisherman's Hall, though it was enjoyed by visiting sailors rather than by islanders. It was intended to provide "Tea, buns and a singsong" for visiting fishermen, especially for the crews of the Manx boats who came in such numbers before World War I. Its real purpose was to keep the crews out of the hotel bar and the public houses and must have contributed to peace and quiet. The Misses Delap and the Misses FitzGerald were the mainstay of its organisers and helpers. They are kindly remembered.

Apart from the sporting activities which were part of the lives of the cable staff, the island had more native activities. Gaelic football was played almost from the foundation of the Gaelic Athletic Association. In 1910 the island team played Waterville and won. Joe Smith (Capt), P. Murphy (goal) W. Higgins, D. Higgins, M. Sugrue, W. Shanahan, J. Jones, M. Neill, P. Casey, T. Lyne, M. Murphy, M. Brosnan, D. Mc Carthy, Edwd. Twohig, T. Shea, J. Burke, and W. Murphy made up the team.

More colourful was the match against a team from the war steamer *Racoon* held on the island in 1886. We do not know what rules were followed but the names of both teams were published in the *Tralee and*

Killarney Echo. The goals were set 106 yards apart and the match went on for over four hours. The Valentia team were adept at sending their opponents sprawling resulting in the comment from the crowd "There's no fun in throwing them red caps, they take it so easy". Valentia scored the only goal, but all must have enjoyed the spectacle because ".. an instance of the good spirit of the play occurred near the end, when Ricks, the Marine drummer, not fully five feet high, closed in with big Charley Murphy. The whole party kept aloof and commenced a roar of laughter at the Irish giant and the English dwarf - Charley good humouredly prolonged the fun by allowing the little fellow to push him about, and at length carrying away the ball as if by chance."

Another entertaining match and a more dangerous one, was against a team of Spaniards from the boats in the harbour held in 1929, before the Spanish Civil war. Spanish boats were a common sight at this period, so that the local fishermen complained that the Spaniards were "tearing up the spawning beds inside the 3 mile limit". Island shopkeepers and oil and petrol agents were glad of the extra business and the islanders in general found the Spaniards friendly. The late Liam McGabhann recalled going for trips on the boats and drinking terrible wine and eating beautiful fruit.

During all the summer of 1929 the Spaniards had strolled around the island while their ships took on water or vegetables or diesel oil, or merely waited for the rough seas to abate. They watched the Valentia football team practising and often if the pitch was not crowded, they would discard their wooden shoes and dribble the ball about with the local team. When a storm brought to the harbour more trawlers than were ever seen, the Spaniards suggested that there were enough footballers among the crews to play a Valentia team in football. When the starting time came the village of Knightstown was a bit surprised to see about two hundred Spaniards going up in groups to the football field at Cracow. The Spaniards even carried their tri-colour with them. The islanders explained in pidgin English and pidgin Spanish that they would not use their hands in the game in deference to the Spaniards, who were not accustomed to fielding the ball. All were to play in socks. Things went smoothly until an Irish player, Pat (Siki) Murphy, shouldered his man. The Spaniard went hurtling in to the ditch and when he came out he was certainly voluble. Kieran O'Driscoll, who was the referee, reckoned that Siki hadn't fouled and signalled the play on.

From the sidelines Spaniards came rushing into the field and the sun glinted on naked knives. The island team were slowly pressed against the fence, still arguing. Before any one could discover whether the sailors would use the knives, there was the report of a shot. One of the Spanish ships' captains had fired a revolver into the air. Other captains drew revolvers and trained the guns on the Spaniards. To add to the excitement, a local man, Jackie Sugrue, who had been watching the match from his own door, arrived dressed in an R.I.C. helmet and tunic, relics left behind by a Concert troupe. He casually swung a shot-gun in his arms. Nobody ever knew whether the Spaniards regarded him as part of a police force but between his gun and those of their officers, they slowly withdrew from the field. The local Gardai then arrived to patrol the pier and sensibly kept the Spaniards out of the village pub.

It was not until the next evening, Sunday, when the Spaniards paid their customary visit to the chapel by the sea, dressed in their Sunday best of blue-sashed pants and stark white shirts, that friendly relations were restored.

Valentia's major claim to fame in the world of football came much later when Michael (Mick) O'Connell became a household name. His style of play has been described as "poetry in motion".

Today there is a substantial pavilion at the Sports Field in Chapeltown. The late Robbie Graves compared conditions now with what he remembered at the beginning of this century when "men fielded, ran and kicked the ball in their normal clothing and caps and usually in their everyday walking boots. Matches were played with spirit, fervour and tenacity, urged on by vociferous enthusiastic spectators in the field beside Cracow".

Sports day was always another big occasion. An early programme preserved among the FitzGerald papers shows the various skills displayed.

Regattas were also very important and races between the local crews and those of visiting Naval boats. On one such occasion the captain of the visiting boat asked that the race should not be held on a Friday as on that day his men would not have had a "feed of meat" and without this they would be unable to perform at their best. The Knight consented but remarked that it would make no difference to his men, as they only ate meat at Christmas and Easter. When the tale was being told later, the narrator remarked that the Knight did not know everything that went on and that the tenants never told the Knight every time they killed a pig.

What made Valentia a "different Irish Island"? Did it fit into the description of the Congested Districts of the West of Ireland given in the Report of the Royal Commission on Local Taxation in 1902? "In the congested districts there are two classes mainly, the poor and the destitute. There are hardly any resident gentry, there are a very few traders and officials, but nearly all the inhabitants are either poor or on the verge of poverty."

Richard Robinson, whose father was a "Radio" man, had very happy memories of growing up on the island in the 1940s. He thinks "that an island has a grip on your heart, and the sea has a grip on your soul and that neither one ever lets go".

Glanleam golf course in 1912.

Chapter 12 - Island Amenities and Sports.

Tennis party with Marquee in front of Cable Houses.

137

Principal Sources

FITZGERALD PAPERS in National Library, Dublin including S.M.2077, 5947-51; National Archives, Four Courts, Dublin, 1901 and 1911 Census, M 2735; FitzGerald family archives, London; County Library, Tralee.

TRINITY COLLEGE LIBRARY. Documents relating to Trinity College Estates. Thesis Dr. Robert Brian McCarthy.

PAPERS RELATING TO TRANS-ATLANTIC CABLE in N.L.I. Larcom Papers. M.7787.In Quaker Library, Donnybrook, Typescript No. 155: 1855-99.

LAND COMMISSION. Schedules of Areas, Inspectors Reports, etc of Congested Districts Board Estates. C.D.B.9953. C.D.B. 10149. Base Line Reports and Digest of Evidence to Board 1908.

ACCOUNTS OF THE GREAT FAMINE in State Paper Office, Dublin Castle. Distress CSORP 1847/8606, D8555, D2264, D1151, D880. British Parliamentry Papers.

ROYAL IRISH ACADEMY DUBLIN. History of Kerry compiled O'Sullivan O.F.M. c. 1750. R.I.A.Ms 24K 43.

FOLKLORE RECORDS, FOLKLORE COMMISSION, University College, Dublin. Vol. 239 and 308.

HERITAGE CENTRE VALENTIA ISLAND. Information about all aspects of island life.

"AN T-OILEANACH" journal published on the island in the 1970s.

CHURCH RECORDS both local Catholic and Church of Ireland.

FREEMASONS RECORDS Moleworth Street, Dublin.

METEOROLOGICAL SERVICE ANNUAL REPORT. 1976.

PUBLISHED WORKS including "A handy book of reference for Irishwomen" by Helen Blackburn. Commisions, Reports and unpublished work including Report of British Association for Relief in Ireland. 1849; Dialann Dairbhre Nov. 1988. Issued by Tessa O'Connor, Valentia Heritage; Account of Maude and Constance Delap; Commissioners of Education Report 1826; Devon Commission 1844; Encumbered Estates Court, Ireland; Island and Coast Society annual reports; Kerry County Joint Technical Instruction Commission Annual Reports; Mines and Minerals Survey 1922; Department of Agriculture Reports; Kerry County Committee of Agriculture Reports; Minutes of Valentia Island Agricultural Bank; Griffith Survey 1852.

NEWSPAPER AND PERIODICAL ARTICLES including Cockroft, Irene. "Used in the mansions of the nobility. The rise and fall of a slate company". Country Life Magazine. Feb.22, 1979; Cornish Telegraph. Jan. 29.1.1925. Article: "Romance of the Sub-marine Cable". Address by Mr. T. O'Donaghue at Penzance; de Cogan, D. " Dr. E.O.W. Whitehouse and the 1858 Trans-Atlantic cable" and other articles; Dickens, Charles. Household Words. No. 136. 30/10/1852. Vol.6 1853; Inniu,1/6/1973; " Risteard O'Glaisne ag comhra leis an mBrathair Peadar;" Irish Builder. 1st July 1882 ;Irish Citizen. 5th Oct. 1912 and 13th Nov. 1915; Short Historical Sketch of the Masonic Lodge No. 130 "Star of the West", Valentia Island,1905; Article. Evening Post. 8th August 1857; National Gazetteer, 1868; D. N. B. Supplement. Information on Helen Blackburn and Bewicke Blackburn; The Dublin Builder. Vol. V.11/12/63, VII No.138. 15/4/1865; Irish Builder 1/8/1882; Telegrapher 1885; Bulletin of Miscellaneous information. Kew 1917. Article on Lecky flower drawings;"Valentia Fireside, yesterday". Capuchin Annual. Article by Nora Ni Shuilliobhain; "Lonely lives", newspaper article about Mrs Sheila Keenan; Irish Home Industries

Association catalogue of goods at Exhibition at Depot 57 Dawson St., March 1888; Journal of the Women's National Health Association 1909, 1910 and 1911; Irish Times 6/11/70. "The long slow death of the Iveragh Gaeltacht;" Office of Public Works. Appendix to first and second reports from Select Committee on Public Works (Irel.) 1835. Vol. 20;"Zelva School, Valentia Island." By Michael Quane. Published Cork Historical and Archeological Society; Kerry Evening Post. 29/6/1910; Mac Gabhann, Liam. Article "Valentia and The Hungry Sea" published Irish Times 10/2/70; Hatton, Helen, Eliz. "The largest amount of good ; Quaker Relief in Ireland" PHD thesis University of Toronto 1988; Tuke, James Hack. N. L.I. Ir. 94108 s 9 F6; Manuscript on growing up in a Cable family in Valentia. The late Robbie Graves' account given to the author; Papers in Commissioner of Irish Lights Offices, Dublin; Delap, Peter. "Memories of a loving alien";Butler, Liam. Dissertation B.A.Hons degree 1989.

ACCOUNTS FROM ISLANDERS AND OTHERS. Mrs Aston, nee Mawe, Father Denis Costello, the Delap family, Adrain FitzGerald, London, Mr and Mrs Richard Foran, Valentia, Mrs Foran Senior, Valentia, the late Robbie Graves, Leo Jones, Lightkeeper, Doreen Kelliher, Dublin (nee O'Sullivan), Mrs Linnane, Knightstown, the late Mrs Margaret Lynch (formerly Graves), Denis Lynch, Tennis, Brother Peadar Lynch, De la Salle Order, Denis Lyne, Jackie McCarthy, Coarhabeg, John McCarthy, Coarhamore, Mrs Molly McCarthy, Coarhamore, Seanie Murphy, Lifeboat Cox and his parents, Sister Catherine O'Connell, the late Mr and Mrs Jeremiah O'Connell, Tessa O'Connor, Mr and Mrs John O'Donoghue, Feaghmaan, Jo. O'Driscoll, Crumlin, Dublin, (Born Dohilla), the late Jeremiah O'Leary, Feaghmaan, Ned and Mary O'Reilly, Mrs Hanoria O'Shea, Coarhabeg, Nora O'Sullivan, Dermot and Clare Ring, Post Office, Knightstown, Richard Robinson, Ennis, Co. Clare, Maura Scannell, Mr and Mrs Brendan Sugrue, Reenglass, Mollie Walsh.

A complete list of the Author's sources are available on written request from the publishers.

KERRY

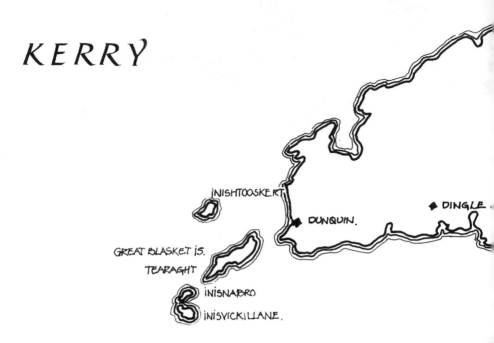

INISHTOOSKERT

GREAT BLASKET IS.

TEARAGHT

DUNQUIN.

♦ DINGLE

INISNABRO

INISVICKILLANE.

CANGLASS
PT.

DOULUS HD.

BEIGINIS

CAH

KEENARD FO

valentia

KNIGHTS
TOWN.

IRELAND

BELFAST.

GALWAY. DUBLIN

LIMERICK

TRALEE. CORK

BRAY
HEAD.

PORTMAGEE.

BALLINSKE

LITTLE SKELLIG.

BOLUS HD.

HOG'S
HEAD.

GREAT SKELLIG.

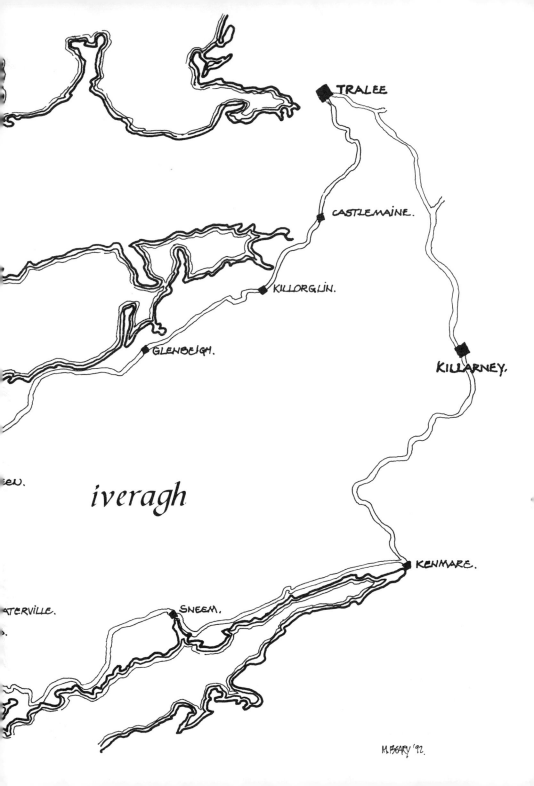

TRALEE

CASTLEMAINE.

KILLORGLIN.

GLENBEIGH.

KILLARNEY.

iveragh

KENMARE.

ATERVILLE.

SNEEM.

M.BEARY '92.

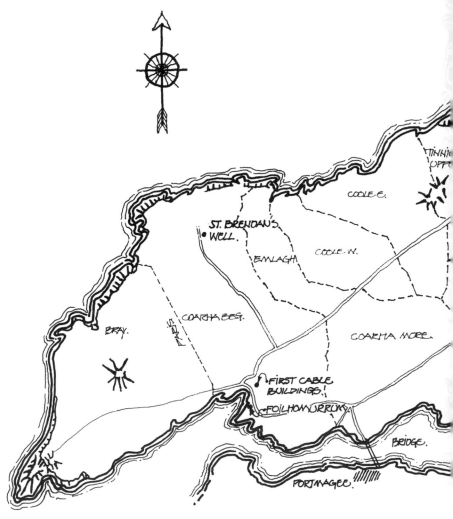

TINNIE
OPP

COOLE E.

ST. BRENDAN'S
WELL.

EMLAGH

COOLE. W.

PRES.

COARHA BEG.

BRAY.

COARHA MORE.

FIRST CABLE
BUILDINGS.

FOILHOMURRUM.

BRIDGE.

PORTMAGEE.

BRAY HEAD.

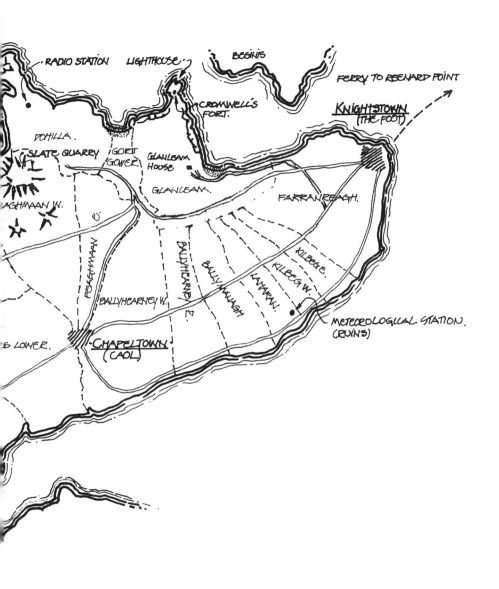

RADIO STATION   LIGHTHOUSE   BEGINIS
FERRY TO REENARD POINT
KNIGHTSTOWN
(THE FOOT)
CROMWELL'S FORT.
DOHILLA.
SLATE QUARRY   GORT (GOWER)
GLANLEAM HOUSE
AGHMAAN W.
GLANLEAM.
FARRANREAGH.
FEAGHMAAN
BALLYHEARNEY
BALLYHEARNEY
KILBEG E.
BALLYHEARNEY W.
BALLYNAUGH
LAHARAN.
KILBEG W.
METEOROLOGICAL STATION.
(RUINS)
S LOWER.
CHAPELTOWN
(CAOL)

VALENTIA ISLAND

M.BEARY '92.

89 | 941-96

RLANN CHONTAE LONGFOIRT
(Longford County Council)

ied for two weeks. Afterwards fines of
week plus any postage incurred will

low is the date by which the b